AF812370

The Language of Economics

Robert E. Mitchell

The Language of Economics

Socially Constructed Vocabularies and Assumptions

palgrave
macmillan

Robert E. Mitchell
Brookline, Massachusetts, USA

ISBN 978-3-319-33980-1 ISBN 978-3-319-33981-8 (eBook)
DOI 10.1007/978-3-319-33981-8

Library of Congress Control Number: 2016943113

© The Editor(s) (if applicable) and the Author(s) 2016
This work is subject to copyright. All rights are solely and exclusively licensed by the Publisher, whether the whole or part of the material is concerned, specifically the rights of translation, reprinting, reuse of illustrations, recitation, broadcasting, reproduction on microfilms or in any other physical way, and transmission or information storage and retrieval, electronic adaptation, computer software, or by similar or dissimilar methodology now known or hereafter developed.
The use of general descriptive names, registered names, trademarks, service marks, etc. in this publication does not imply, even in the absence of a specific statement, that such names are exempt from the relevant protective laws and regulations and therefore free for general use.
The publisher, the authors and the editors are safe to assume that the advice and information in this book are believed to be true and accurate at the date of publication. Neither the publisher nor the authors or the editors give a warranty, express or implied, with respect to the material contained herein or for any errors or omissions that may have been made.

Cover illustration: © Melisa Hasan

Printed on acid-free paper

This Palgrave Macmillan imprint is published by Springer Nature
The registered company is Springer International Publishing AG Switzerland

To two remarkable, supportive, and loving friends
Sylvia Sheppard Mitchell, 1930–1998, for four-plus loving decades of mutually rewarding togetherness. I owe her much.
Riva Blevitzky Berkovitz, 1928–2014, a truly understanding, supportive, and wonderful late-in-life living-apart-together super-intelligent teacher and loving partner.

Preface

This is a book about how the language used by economists shapes their understanding of inequality, a topic attracting much recent attention by economists and others. Although economists will hopefully benefit from the following chapters, all readers should be aware that this is not an Econ 101–type text. Some academics might assign this book to the bookshelves of *Philology*.[1]

But why *inequality*, a term with both descriptive and moral overtones that can become confused in analyses of the phenomenon? Other authors will provide their own answers. Mine come at least in part from what I learned from others about what is fair or not. But, yes, like so many others, I strive to escape from my inherited prejudices, although I am not always successful. For example, at age 86, I am two inches shorter and 5–10 pounds heavier than I was 65 years earlier. Those are the facts of my long life, like them or not.

Not all facts are likeable or fair. Children certainly complain about what is fair or not. Fairness implies some standard of what is acceptable, not what actually exists.

Fairness also implies the need for a standard, a mental marker of what is expected and acceptable.

My own subjective standards shaped how I understood and reacted to what I experienced daily during my decades of living and working in Asia, the Near East, and Africa. To my biased mind, too many of my fellow humans were living an unsatisfactory and unacceptable existence. More than once I would tell myself: There but for the grace of god go I. My neighbors were living the expected but certainly not what was acceptable.

I was then and continue today to be a prisoner of my own values.

But did providence deprive my fellow humans with a lack of grace while rewarding me with what I no doubt did not earn or deserve?

According to most economists, grace has nothing to do with the chasm that separates me or you, the reader, from our fellow human beings. Instead, I was fortunate in living where I could use my limited skills to maneuver through a modern market system, one still struggling to be born in the countries where I resided and served. The lesson, I was told, was to cast aside providential design. God is dead. Only the market counts.

But markets are not empty vessels. They are claimed to be rule-bound systems that, once the rules are discovered, allow the players in this captive vessel to advantage themselves while at the same time contribute to the welfare of all. Modern markets with hidden rules work their miracles. Unfortunately, during much of my career, I was working in a supposedly heathen world of premodern economic men. At least that is how some critics would mischaracterize my perpetual poverty of personal enlightenment.

There is nothing fair about the rules of a modern economy. They are just there, and all of us are rowing the galley of progress and failure. Hallelujah! Both winners and laggards reap what they deserve, so some claim.

Economists are among the many who are dedicated to discovering the laws of an impersonal market, ones that largely lie hidden from our only mortal eyes. Those laws explain why some countries are poor while others are not, why some market players are well-off while others are not. Justice has nothing to do with what markets are or should be. Laws of markets and economies exist, just as the laws of physics just exist. They simply had to await enlightened economists to discover them. And once that was accomplished, market players and processes opened themselves to the use of algebraic formulae, unlike the invisible laws of providential design.

Fortunately, we have benefited from centuries of insightful and creative miners of the market. Standard college economics textbooks organize the accumulated wisdom of generations of academics and practical men who successfully maneuvered through good market times and bad.

Modern economics incorporates a system of definitions, propositions, and theories, all discovered over the past two centuries or so.

"Discovered" is another word for "invented." Yes, economics is a rigorous socially constructed discipline. The Harvard economist Dani Rodrik agrees: "preferences and behavioral patterns are 'socially constructed,' or imposed by the structure of society."[2]

Of course, not all explorers followed the same maps or came up with the identical laws of markets.

Again, this is not a textbook on economics. Instead, it is a book about some of the hidden value assumptions behind the language of the discipline. It is an intellectual and epistemological history that explores and elaborates a limited number of key inequality-related terms, concepts, and mental images invented by centuries of very creative economists and many others.

The same kind of nontechnical history could be authored on how political scientists, sociologists, psychologists, and others also think. All these disciplines, as well as those in the basic sciences and humanities, view the world through their own specialized inherited language lenses.

Members of the various social sciences and humanities will hopefully find this book to be relevant to an understanding of their own disciplines.

We begin with the often-alleged parent of modern economics: Adam Smith, an ingenious inventor of market images and words well before factual evidence and numbers became available to ground-test the new vocabulary of economics. Many of the assumptions made by Smith and those who followed him were based on not-so-hidden values. Alternative values with supporting evidence might have suggested laws different from what we now have in modern economics.

Later chapters introduce the recent attention given to measures and meanings of inequality, a focus given new empirical meaning by Thomas Piketty and others who will be mentioned. Some of the more recent writings on inequality are footnotes to Piketty's masterpiece. While drawing on different historical and value perspectives, they generally buy into the way economists think and their theories.

The present book breaks out of the discipline's accepted paradigm in a number of ways that begin with the unquestioned value-laden vocabulary of economics, the discipline's failure to incorporate the contributions of other social sciences and humanities, and the challenges that mass-data analysts are creating for traditional economics. So in addition to reframing the entire field of inequality, I tie my book to "the end of economics," at least as we have known it. Some new or alternative ways of understanding modern economies, markets, and our world in general are introduced.[3]

Readers no doubt differ in how they find their way through a book. Chapter titles are not always adequate road maps. For this reason, you will hopefully find the rather extended outline below as a way to guide you through the following pages.

Again, I emphasize that what follows is an intellectual and epistemological history that explores a very limited number of key terms, concepts, and mental images invented by centuries of economists. The same kind of nontechnical history could be authored on how political scientists, sociologists, psychologists, and others also think.

From the very beginning of this oldest of the social science disciplines, the vocabulary of economics included terms that have both factual (descriptive) and implied moral meanings. Rational economic man, the invisible hand, natural liberty, equilibrium, demand, and supply are among the many examples of tags that have mixed meanings. Of course, the same observation can be made for the other social sciences—for example, democracy, human rights, freedom, social structure, culture, id, ego, insanity, personality, and normal.

This book's early chapters lay the basis for a consideration of "inequality," one of the major topics currently attracting attention from economists and many others. "Inequality" can be described statistically, as will be done. But the term is burdened with the moral overhang of something that is not necessarily essential or certainly "fair." This mixture of facts and values is not peculiar to economics: it is found in all the social sciences and humanities.

Mixing facts with values is not limited to considerations of inequality. They are also found in the very end goal that economies are to achieve: adding to the wealth of the nation and to the wealth of those who create this wealth. But what to count as wealth involves value decisions, as will be seen.

An important end that economies are to achieve and the measures of progress toward that end are slanted by value decisions made by economists over the decades. And since "inequality" is measured by value-influenced statistical measures, we can see why this term can be politically explosive.

Inequality is not a term reserved for economic analysis alone. Historians and other social scientists have written on hierarchies in general, why they exist, and what they supposedly do. Some of this work is reviewed in later chapters.

The book's long historical perspective reminds us that words included in the dictionaries of the social sciences often date back to societies and economies that are very different from what we have today. Old dictionaries and mental models based on a mass production economy can blind analysts from understanding modern knowledge-based systems. Chapter 8 in this book briefly covers some of the recent alternatives to dated economic thinking based on old value-based dictionaries invented by long-ago economists.

The future may be influenced by the ability of economists and others to think outside the mental boxes of this oldest of the modern social sciences.

Although this is definitely not a traditional book on economics, members of this discipline and others should find much that is relevant to an understanding of their respective field's proud past and likely near future.

To help identify that relevance, each chapter begins with several indented paragraphs that place the chapter's materials in a larger social science and humanities context.

Here is what I hope will be a useful road map to follow in reading this book's eight chapters.

Chapter 1: Economists' Epistemological Challenges

"Socially constructed languages" are a widely used mode of analysis among members of both the humanities and the social sciences. Keynes drew on some of this same analytical tradition, as have recent books on economics by Jonathan Schlefer and Florian Schui. Chapter 1 draws on the social construction perspective used by humanists and some social scientists in order to understand the Alice-in-Wonderland vocabulary of economics by:

(1) introducing a few invented vocabulary terms and assumptions found in the historical writings of economists,
(2) raising questions about this vocabulary and the assumptions behind individual words,
(3) identifying some of the questions raised about the epistemology of this now-well-established and rightfully respected discipline, and
(4) explaining why this is a book about the moral basis of economic thinking rather than a now-traditional book on economics and markets.

We will see why economists, like the rest of us, are prisoners of their own vocabularies. The language of economics directs members of the discipline to what to study and how to think. In these respects, economists are no different from theologians, social scientists, and you the reader.

Chapter 2: The Trajectory of the First Social Science

Rather than beginning with the earliest economists, this chapter starts with the current diversity within the discipline: the subspecialties, competing ideological camps, and contrasting value assumptions.

Some leading economists recognize that their discipline is based on value assumptions and myths that talking heads and advocacy centers promote. Adam Smith and those who followed him invented mythical mental models of markets, economic man, and the invisible hand before factual evidence was available to ground test these newly invented vocabularies and mental models.

This chapter ends with the question to be pursued in follow-on chapters: if all economists use the same economics-speak, facts, and numbers, why are there differences in how inequality is understood and explained?

Chapter 3: An Overview of Socially Constructed Mental Models and Vocabularies

According to Erving Goffman, "We frame reality in order to negotiate it, manage it, comprehend it, and choose appropriate repertories of cognition and actions." This chapter explores the what and why of mental models in general as well as why the language of economics adopted such terms as rational economic man and the invisible hand. Although rational economic man may have been a rare endangered species, he was an essential component of models of modern markets. This rare breed was invented by Enlightenment thinkers, some of whom added "virtue" as an extramarket force to control the selfish pursuer of personal wealth. Bernard Mandeville made contrary assumptions about economic man but arrived at the same end result that Adam Smith invented: additions would be made to the wealth of the nation.

Our contemporary behavioral economists have shown the fallacy of rational economic man and the invisible hand. Even earlier, Milton Friedman suggested that the accuracy of economists' predictions trumped the need for assumptions behind the actions of market players. Some of the implications of this contrary view are explored in this and later chapters.

Chapter 4: From Metaphor to Fact: The Early History of Creating a New Language of Markets and Economies

This largely historical chapter draws on recent studies of how economists attempt to create order out of the unknown. To do this required the invention of general categories, facts to represent these categories, and ways to count and interpret the numbered facts. Adam Smith and others were following Isaac Newton in using mathematical laws to explain order in both markets and the societies in which they operated. The assumed laws and markers (evidence) required facts that could be numbered, the mark of a true science.

Some of the questions pursued in this chapter include: What is a fact, that is, a fact about markets and economies, not just individual economic men? How does one move from metaphor and conjecture to fact? What if any value and moral assumptions impinge on mentally created economic images and facts? What is wealth and why does it play such a central role in economics? What are the units and measures of wealth (e.g., prices and quantities)? What units other than wealth might be considered but not yet accepted? Why some measures rather than others? How does the selection of basic units shape the way economists think? What is overlooked, if anything, when the focus is on wealth, its creation, and its creators? Who has the say on what are facts and how to understand them? Why some facts rather than others? Several other questions are also explored in this and later chapters.

Separate attention is given to claims made for and against the invisible hand and the operation of the price system. Based on the questions raised and answers to them, the chapter explores the charge that economics is a pseudoscience drowning in "mathiness." Despite the criticisms leveled against traditional economics, there are creative economists who continue to peddle conclusions based on questionable assumptions. One example is hazarded.

Chapter 5: Value Judgments Regarding the Meaning of Wealth

Everyone presumably wants to add to the nation's wealth. To know whether forward progress is being made toward that goal, it is necessary to define what wealth means and its key components so that facts and measures (numbers) can be assembled. Other decisions are also necessary. For example, economists are challenged to clarify what they mean by the economy, why some features (categories) are important measures of the stock of wealth, and the key drivers behind changes in this stock. Addressing these conceptual and measurement challenges requires value as well as analytical decisions, all guided by the assumed purposes or rationale for focusing on economies and changes in them.

This chapter explores some of the not-so-hidden value assumptions made in selecting measures for the socially constructed concept of national wealth (income and product). Some of the issues explored are: What to measure and whether measures invented for a mass production economy are relevant to the knowledge-based one we now have.

We begin this exploration with a question raised by an American sociologist three decades ago:

> "At issue in the design of national accounts are fundamental questions of policy, not just of fact. In the early debate over the accounts, Simon Kuznets repeatedly emphasized the practical impossibility of measuring national product without making philosophical choices about the end-purpose of economic activity…estimators had no choice but to make explicit philosophical choices." Moreover, "[o]fficial statistics do not merely hold a mirror to reality. They reflect presuppositions and theories about the nature of reality. They are products of social, political, and economic interests that are often in conflict with each other. And they are sensitive to methodological decisions made by complex organizations with limited resources. Moreover, official numbers, especially those that appear in series, often do not reflect all these factors instantaneously: They echo their past as the surface of a landscape reflects its underlying geology."

Measures of economic health require decisions about the end goal of economies and polities. Economic welfare, according to some observers, is more than just economic "outputs." There are alternative measures of national welfare that, according to some experts, better measure welfare than the measures used in the recent past and those that Adam Smith assumed to be most important. Old ideologies, however, still have a powerful hold on American politics, as seen in the price paid by major economists and the statistics establishment that questioned President Reagan's management of the economy.

Chapter 6: Alternative Values and Mental Models: The Recurring Challenge of Inequality

This chapter explores some alternatives to Adam Smith's goal of adding to the wealth of the nation. In contrast to Smith's assumption about increasing prosperity, what Thomas Malthus saw "were not signs of progressive improvement but human suffering and pain." French observers at the same time saw "a perpetual oscillation between happiness and misery."

Malthus, according to the literary historian Mary Poovey, advocated "a combination of induction and reasoning from religious principles as the best means of assessing national well-being" and that "the science of political economy bears a nearer resemblance to the science of morals and politics than to that of mathematics." Values could not be expunged from the economist's vocabulary. That is a hard pill for most economists to swallow.

Malthus evidently lost the debate, but the reincarnation of poverty over time failed to disappear. It has been recently rediscovered under the catchword "inequality," not just the absence of basic necessities and Franklin D. Roosevelt's "freedom from want."

This chapter begins to ask why societies inhabited by rational economic men continue to suffer from high rates of poverty and increasing inequality. Some economists and others argue that markets must be placed in the larger social, political, and cultural systems in which they operate. Each of these systems has its own constellation of values and offices responsible for honoring them. Yet economics still occupies a favored position in the struggle to understand and manage contemporary life so that all members of society benefit. Values and the power behind them still matter.

Chapter 7: The Long-Standing Interest in the Meanings, Causes, and Consequences of Inequality

Thomas Piketty and others have rekindled an interest in how to measure and explain changing profiles of inequality, a term that has both statistical and socially constructed value-laden meanings. Among other topics, this chapter covers:

1. Piketty's justly well-received historical review of international differences in "economic" inequality over time. Our focus is limited to the American experience.

2. How selected other economists, historians, and social scientists have viewed inequality.
3. Claims made by moral philosophers and social scientists that some patterns of inequality are neither natural nor necessary. They are results of policy choices that have been made in the past.
4. Shifting from moral values and economics, the chapter looks at the ways that some analysts have understood how politics, policies, and power have influenced the patterns and consequences of inequality.
5. Inequality, according to some observers, is to be celebrated, not criticized. We look at some of these apologies and apologists.
6. How the founding father of modern economics, Adam Smith, viewed the forces behind the inequality of his own time.
7. The focus shifts from economists to other social scientists who addressed the origins and meanings of inequality.
8. Based on the above, the chapter closes with questions that contemporary economists and others are asking about inequality and the future of economics.

This chapter also places the specific term "inequality" within the context of a more general category of "hierarchy," an image well studied by sociologists and political scientists. We will see that hierarchies are also shadowed by value assumptions.

Chapter 8: Is the Past a Reliable Prologue for the Future of Economics?

Yes, economists have greatly added to our understanding of the forces that drive changes in the world's many economies. But the discipline is inhabited by competing value assumptions, ideological objectives, and discarded laws (such as Say's law). One critic claimed that "even if there are laws of economics, we haven't been observing them for long enough to know what they actually are. And given the vagaries of human behavior and the mercurial nature of states, people and institutions, the notion that there's some grand mechanistic, master system that explains all and predicts everything is at best a comforting fiction and at worst a straitjacket that precludes creativity, forestalls innovation and destroys dynamism. Referencing 'the laws of economics' as a way to refute arguments or criticize ideas has the patina of clarity and certainty. The reality is that referencing such laws is simply another way to justify beliefs and inclinations."

This chapter introduces some recent alternatives to traditional economics as a way to understand how a knowledge-based society differs from one based on mass production. "Social learning," according to some recent analysts, needs to replace the individual rational market player. For example, Alex Pentland, author of *Social Physics*, argued that "[i]n our new hyperconnected world, most [social and economic] ties are weak, and all too often the invisible hand no longer functions." Instead of the "old vocabulary of markets and class, capital and production," economists need to recognize that people and markets move more than goods and money: the flow of information and ideas is even more important today. Instead of focusing primarily on rational thinking, one must understand how social networks (the social context abandoned by economists when political economy was replaced by economics alone) operate.

Pentland's social physics and network analysis has a fairly long history in the sociology of knowledge that researches the diffusion of information and the adoption of innovations. Robert K. Merton and his colleague Paul F. Lazarsfeld contributed to this supplement to traditional economics and sociology.

This chapter explores some of the justifications for this supplement to mainline economics. But old economic theories, like some old soldiers, do not quietly go away. In fact, despite the many criticisms of rational economic man, this creature has infiltrated the other social sciences. This chapter notes two rational-man incursions into noneconomic spheres.

Perhaps all of us should heed Joan Robinson's advice: "The Purpose of studying economics is not to acquire a set of ready-made answers to economic questions, but to learn how to avoid being deceived by economists."

Notes

1. For an excellent recent history of this specialty, see James Turner, *Philology: The Forgotten Origins of the Modern Humanities* (Princeton, 2014). Others might put this book in the same genre represented by authors such as John Gray, someone whom the present author is intellectually incapable of replicating. Deirdre McCloskey has several challenging books on how economists use language. See her *The Rhetoric of Economics* (University of Wisconsin, 1998) and *Bourgeois Dignity: Why Economics Can't Explain the Modern World* (Chicago, 2014).
2. Dani Rodrik, *Economics Rules: The Rights and Wrongs of the Dismal Society* (Norton, 2015), 181. He was criticizing methodological individualism

among other assumptions that economists make. He also claims: "Economics is a *social* science, which means that the search for universal theories and results is futile." (p. 183)

3. One of my earlier titles to this book included "the end of economics" rather than "to the future of the discipline."

Contents

CHAPTER 1

Economists' Epistemological Challenges

Abstract Literary and other sources illustrate the meanings of "social construction" and its place in modern economics. Economic dictionaries are inhabited by invented words that mix value with factual components. The former can blind analysts from understanding markets. Economists, just like the rest of us, are prisoners of their vocabularies and become marionettes who are directed on both what and how to think.

It is a challenge to think outside one's own socially constructed disciplinary box, although there are escapees.

Keywords Socially constructed • Epistemology • Vocabulary

We live in a real economy as well as in the Alice in Wonderland that is inhabited by images and mental models invented by economists over the centuries. Of course, when the world changed, so did the socially constructed language used to understand and manage markets and economies. Yes, economists and others significantly contributed to our understanding of markets and what drives them. At the same time, some of this understanding is based on conjectures and values inherited from the far and more recent past.

But old dictionaries, like old soldiers, never die; they just fade away.[1] Some don't even do that. They have a lasting influence on what we see and what we understand. We can easily become prisoners of our vocabularies; we are their marionettes.

© The Editor(s) (if applicable) and the Author(s) 2016

R.E. Mitchell, *The Language of Economics*,
DOI 10.1007/978-3-319-33981-8_1

Vocabularies, of course, are absolutely essential, for they help answer the basic epistemological question of how we know what we know. We cannot even ask questions without using language. We are surrounded by and dependent on symbols.

Each discipline and profession has its own technical language that members must master. This is not just for medical doctors and lawyers but also for economists. *The Oxford Dictionary of Economics* (2009 edition) defines 2500 key economic terms. The eight-volume set of *The New Palgrave Dictionary of Economics* (2008) runs to 7344 pages, with 5.7 million words in 1900 different articles authored by some 1500 eminent contributors.

Student-economists can drown in the thousands of meanings they are mandated to memorize.

Economists, however, are not unique. Psychology, political science, geography, and sociology have their own specialized vocabularies that instruct their respective members on how to view and understand the world. And the same holds for members of the clergy: *The Oxford Dictionary of World Religions* (1997) has 1136 pages of terms and explanations. There are other dictionaries and encyclopedias specific to the multitude of individual faiths, Christian and many others.

Religious dictionaries are not unique in mixing factual, historical, and value-based assumptions. They help practitioners and others to filter and organize the world around them. This is certainly true for economists as well.

Learning a discipline's or trade's language is an essential rite de passage in one's educational and career trajectory.[2] Swallow, accept, memorize, and move on. What you swallow, however, might be poison in the near future, as Chris Beneke suggested in his review article on "the coercive moral establishment in the early (American) republic."

> Describing the impact of early republican religious culture, Alexis de Tocqueville observed that Americans could not conceive—could not bring to cognition—what their Christian faith wouldn't allow them. They were "obliged to profess an ostensible respect for Christian morality and equity…" As bold as they were in enterprise, Tocqueville thought these people were meek in matters of the intellect.[3]

Economists who represent competing schools of analysis strive, it seems, to dominate our contemporary moral universe. Shared as well as disputed, analytical and moral philosophies held by those within the discipline can compete with and overlap one another. Economic dictionaries may list the same words but not the same meanings assigned to them.

Moreover, the language of economics can be quite quickly dated so that members of this discipline no longer have an adequate window into understanding contemporary life. Language itself is part of the problem. Still, members of all professions and trades must learn the dictionary entrees ordained by their discipline. They must also delearn the fallacies of earlier vocabularies that were born in the evil predisciplinary world of Sodom and Gomorrah.

Modern economists beckon us to their discipline's Garden of Eden. Yes, lots of moral overtones and assumptions can be found in the holy dictionaries of modern economics.[4]

Economists and others attuned to the importance of language will surely recognize themselves in this Mother Goose rhyme that Karl N. Llewellyn used in his lectures to incoming first-year students in pre–World War II Columbia University's Law School. Student-lawyers must unlearn an old language while memorizing a new one:

> There *was a man in our town,*
> *And he was wondrous wise,*
> *He jumped into a bramble bush,*
> *And scratched out both his eyes;*
> *But when he saw his eyes were out,*
> *With all his might and main,*
> *He jumped into another bush,*
> *And scratched 'em in again.*[5]

This introductory chapter begins a long journey that

(1) introduces a few vocabulary terms and assumptions found in the historical writings of economists,
(2) begins to raise questions about this vocabulary and the assumptions behind individual words,
(3) identifies some of the questions raised about the epistemology of this now-well-established and rightfully respected discipline, and
(4) explains why this is a book about the moral basis of economic thinking rather than a now-traditional book on economics and markets.

Later chapters will give special attention to how economists understood the now-common value (and empirical) term *inequality*.

Yes, economists have contributed much to our understanding of the world, but this understanding often rests on questionable conjectures, assumptions, and values. They, economists, like the rest of us, are prisoners of our dictionaries and the hidden values we inherit from the past.

We Are Prisoners of Our Dictionaries

There is always the danger that our vocabularies become iron cages that blind us to what is really happening in an ever-changing world. Habitual ways of thinking, as will be revisited later, need not be rational thinking.

It is now somewhat passé to explore how the vocabularies and mental models of past imaginary worlds shape our understanding of the present. Winston Churchill, for example, spoke before the House of Commons in 1943: "We shape our buildings, and afterwards our buildings shape us." Vocabularies are like buildings: they are created and then shape those who later follow the creators. That is also one of the intended consequences of knowing one's holy books.

The House of Commons, the building that shaped the world of Churchill, had a long architectural, institutional, and social history, as did the associated English polity with its rich legacy that includes the effects that the Scottish and English Enlightenments had on how the English-speaking world understood itself over time.

The early Enlightenment innovators were moral philosophers. But when some thinkers began to focus more on the changing economy of England and the world, moral philosophy was institutionally relabeled as political economy only to be renamed by Alfred Marshall as economics and economics only.

Names may change, but dictionaries, values, and mental models have a long shelf life. They can hide as well as shine understanding on the current world in which we now live.

It can be helpful to recognize that early moral philosophers, political economists, and economists lived in an evidence and number-poor world. Authors had to invent new words, refurbish old ones, and imagine mental models using these words. Once invented, these models and their vocabularies shaped how the world is understood. But the world and its economies change over time. As a result, mental models and vocabularies can soon mask significant transformations and current challenges.

Unfortunately, as William Faulkner observed: "The past is never dead. It's not even past." However, any review of older economists' writings indicates that as economies and societies changed, so did some of the vocabularies invented to understand and manage markets. "Progress" or change was recognized. Still, although one might assume that "old think" would have a decent burial, that has not always happened in the discipline of economics. The vocabulary of economics is still inhabited by aardvark-like words, concepts, and mental models, some of which can too easily mask questionable values and assumptions, as we will explore in later chapters.

Again, economists have their own rich language and vocabulary that can be found in the discipline's standard dictionaries. But let us place these dictionaries in a larger context.

As George Orwell argued, political language, a peculiar patois, "is designed to make lies sound truthful and murder respectable, and to give an appearance of solidity to pure wind." Some (certainly not all) of economic language terms warrant the same indictment. This seems especially so among nonacademic polemical economists peddling their bespoken imperatives from the halls of ideologically driven think tanks.[6]

Orwell gave advice that at least some economists accepted: "Never use a metaphor, simile, or other figure of speech which you are used to seeing in print." In his *Nineteen Eighty-Four*, he introduced "Newspeak," a controlled language created by the totalitarian state Oceania as a tool to narrow the range (freedom) of thought. Any form of thought alternative to the party's construct is classified as "thoughtcrime."

Controlling what are acceptable paradigms and languages can itself become a tool to control how we think about markets and the agents within them.

Some critics might charge economists (some but not all of them) with viewing the world through rose-colored glasses that distort reality in ways to benefit some while harming others. Thomas Kuhn, for example, saw the consequences that scientific language can have. He argued that structures of power are embedded in structures of thought. Which claims about "truth" hold sway depends on what mental models one accepts.

Some economic and social models leave less room than others for selected policy initiatives. For example, some functionalist theories in sociology and anthropology, as well as economics, seem to assume that modern markets and societies are self-correcting systems that do not and should not be targets for reform. Que Sera, Sera.

Dictionaries of economics and economic textbooks can become a form of Economics-speak analogous to Newspeak. This is true, of course, for texts used in other disciplines as well, for economics is certainly not unique. All probably have their equivalents to Orwell's bellyfeel, blackwhite, crimethink, duckspeak, goodsex, sexcrime, ownlife, and unperson. These are not descriptive but instead prescriptive words with not-so-hidden values that are perhaps not too different from economic-speak's use of perfect markets, wealth, rational economic man, and the invisible hand. Once we accept (internalize) these words, we can become marionettes of our language, as John Gray argued. The marionette is controlled by the puppeteers, and "A puppet has no soul. As a result it cannot know it is unfree." Analogously, we are not free of our dictionaries. We are their slaves.[7]

The words that economists use presumably both reflect and create knowledge systems that shape how we view, understand, and miss the meanings of the real world in which we live.

To noneconomists, such as myself, some of the wonderful inventions made by economists seem not too different from Lewis Carroll's Alice in Wonderland world.

I have already introduced the twin descriptive term "mental model" several times. But what does it really mean?

I attempted a shorthand description in my earlier *A Concise History of Economists' Assumptions About Markets*:

> It loosely refers to a simplified abstract framework that identifies relationships among both *observed concrete evidence* and assumed (or abstract) *processes*. A mental model is an argumentative framework that attempts to provide a simplified representation of some feature of the past, present, and future worlds. (Note the repeated use of *simplified*.)[8]

How to Think, Not Just What to Think

We are surrounded by mental models that are often imaginary worlds that are both inviting nirvanas as well as Dante's seven levels of suffering and spiritual growth (associated with the seven deadly sins). Adam Smith's imaginary free market economy was a nirvana; the command economy under Russian communism was a real-life purgatory. Each of these contrasting worlds was populated by imaginary (and real) economic men and women, not necessarily unlike you, the reader of this sentence.

Fortunately historians, linguists, and even economists are beginning to place contemporary economic words, concepts, and assumed value biases in an historical context. Mary Poovey, among others, has written on the historical development of economic dictionaries, conjectures, facts, and not-so-hidden biases. Her *A History of the Modern Fact: Problems of Knowledge in the Sciences of Wealth and Society*[9] and *Genres of the Credit Economy: Mediating Value in Eighteenth-and Nineteenth-Century Britain*[10] explain how key terms, metaphors, images, conjectures, and mental models were "operationalized" as facts that could be counted (numbers became important) and combined with other numbered facts to create evidence-based hypotheses and models of markets and economies more generally.

Poovey provides a new history of the development of the language of economics, the sources of new words and concepts, rhetorical battles between different schools of thought, and some of the roads not taken. She, however, is not alone in noting that economists throughout the ages have been inventing history, not just recording it.

Facts certainly do not add up to history, as Immanuel Wallerstein and others noted for decades.[11] Our knowledge and truths are "social creations" that we use to understand the world, including markets and economies. That is one of the reasons why it is helpful to understand the history of the history of economics—or any discipline.

We are taught not just what to think but also how to think. Thinking, as Poovey and epistemologists argue, is filtered through the vocabularies that earlier generations created in response to their efforts to understand the worlds of their time. As times changed, new words were added to the analysts' vocabularies—but old words seem to hang on, as will be noted again later.

My own *A Concise History of Economists' Assumptions about Markets: From Adam Smith to Joseph Schumpeter* explores how and why major early economists identified a limited number of forces believed to drive markets and economies toward adding to the wealth of a nation.[12] Wealth was the *end* objective of markets and the yardstick for assessing movement toward that objective. For example, Adam Smith titled Chapter 1 in Book 3 of his *The Wealth of Nations*: The Natural Progress of Opulence.[13] Adding to opulence (wealth) was the raison d'être of markets. It was a standard for assessing the value-laden term "progress."

Although the distribution of wealth could possibly influence progress toward the eventual nirvana, "fair" distribution was not an end in itself.

The distribution of the rewards from trucking and trading did not attract the attention of economists. It was a secondary issue primarily of concern to reformers and their soft-hearted sympathizers. (More on this in later chapters.)

Other authors—for example, Lawrence Freedman in his *Strategy, A History* (Oxford, 2013)—place a variety of mental models and dictionaries in a broader social (and military) context that includes descriptions of human motivations during biblical times. In so doing, questions can be asked about core economic- and social-life assumptions (e.g., about rational economic man) made by economists from Adam Smith on. And the challenges of "inequality" raise questions about the central role that economists have placed on increasing a nation's total national wealth rather than how that wealth is distributed. More on this also in two later chapters.

There is nothing natural or god-given about distribution or inequality: both are results of policy decisions, or at least implied decisions taken or not.[14]

The disciplinary train of economists hauls ideological baggage along with what is truly very useful. And that train continues on: new terms are occasionally added to the discipline's dictionary of terms, metaphors, and mental models.

Economists, of course, have been aware of poverty in the midst of plenty. For example, perhaps based on his walks through the slums of Manchester, Alfred Marshall discovered:

> [C]onditions which surround extreme poverty…tend to deaden the higher faculties. Those who have been called the Residuum of our large towns have little opportunity for friendship; they know nothing of the decencies and the quiet, and very little even of the unity of family life; and religion often fails to reach them. No doubt their physical, mental, and moral ill-health is partly due to other causes than poverty: but this is the chief cause…
>
> Now at last we are setting ourselves seriously to inquire whether it is necessary that there should be any so-called "lower classes" at all…

Marshall then asked

> the question whether it is really impossible that all should start in the world with a *fair*[15] chance of leading a cultured life, free from the pains of poverty and the stagnating influences of excessive mechanical toil…The question cannot be fully answered by economic science. For the answer depends partly on the moral and political capabilities of human nature, and on these matters the economist has no special means of information: he must do as others do, and guess as best he can. But the answer depends in a great measure upon facts and inferences, which are within the province of economics; and this it is which gives to economic studies their chief and their highest interest.

Marshall concluded that the "condition of the working classes in England became more gloomy" in the recent past. That was not good for workers, their families, marriages, and children. But the lack of cultured life and the benefits it provides was not a gap that economics or economists could alone fill. Economists were to keep their eye single, which many continue to do. Economists don't deal with feelings and values relating to them (with exceptions to be explored later).

Instead of defining the problem as one related to inequality, Marshall focused on poverty and the ethically driven question of how to raise the poor to the level of an English gentleman. This lifting would require an increase in worker productivity, the economist's answer. There was nothing wrong with the larger system. The fault lay with the laggards within it. Improving their lot would require skills that new technologies needed. An educated workforce would minimize poverty and turn workers into gentlemen, who then would have the same mores of Marshall's own social circle.[16]

Marshall converted poverty and the values held by the poor into a focused concern with worker skills and training that employers would or should welcome. Stark inequality was a natural result of personal and vocational deficiencies, not something that social reformers could improve.

Marshall provided an economist's answer to an economist's question. Some of our more contemporary scholars are following a different route by, for example, asking the old epistemological question of how do we know what we know about poverty and, yes, inequality, whatever inequality means?

That question recognizes that the biblical Moses and those who both preceded and followed him did not lay down immutable economic laws about markets, poverty, and inequality. Nor, as will be suggested later, did Adam Smith provide an analytical blueprint and accompanying vocabulary adequate for an understanding of inequality in our contemporary economies. To contribute to this understanding would require borrowing from the dictionaries invented by and for other disciplines. Then, economics would cross a line and thereby lose its lofty disciplinary uniqueness, or so it might seem.

One of Adam Smith's enduring legacies is his vocabulary of market-related words. However, because of the absence of relevant evidence, he necessarily made conjectures about the basic activity units of markets (rational economic men trucking and trading with one another). His imaginary true market required an imaginary economic man to energize it.

If the metaphorical economic man is rational, then metaphorical markets are rational as well, or so it seems to have been assumed when reifying from a lower-level unit (individual rational economic man) to a higher-level abstraction (rationally operating markets). The two went together.[17]

Enlightenment thinkers were certainly creative. Some talking heads today, as we will see later when the findings of Kahneman are introduced, suffer an illusion of being reliable truth-talking pundits rather than ideologues who use old-talk and assumptions to soothsay the future. Moreover, as we will also suggest later, rational economic man may no longer be a realistic unit on which to build mental models of markets and economies. And the very concept of the wealth of a nation is built on value assumptions and decisions, as will be clearly seen in a brief overview of how wealth, as measured by Gross National Product (GNP), evolved over time (Chap. 5).

Questions raised about the assumption of rationality will be covered in two separate chapters, first in Chap. 3, where the focus is on some of the criticisms that behavioral and other economists have leveled against this concept. Here, the focus is on empirical research, whereas Chap. 4 looks back in the early history of economics to suggest why the myth of rationality was socially invented. Two different perspectives with a common conclusion, as will be suggested.

To the degree that man is rational, then it seems reasonable to formalize rules of rationality and to express these rules in standard axiomatic formats so that the language of mathematics can become the language of economics. However, as also will be suggested, some economists believe that these rules need not assume an underlying rationality. The rules expressed in equations are useful in themselves (as though they were expressions of providential design).

So Much for Generalities

The following short chapters will draw on the work of various historians and other scholars who have explored the social construction of the language of economics. Particular attention is given to Adam Smith and other founding fathers of modern economics. This is done in Chap. 2 and others. Several later chapters identify the values that seem to underlie measures of an economy's total operation, as reflected in such concepts as GNP, supposedly analogous to individual "welfare" elevated to a national total and appropriately distributed to all members of a society (Chap. 5). The short

Chaps. 6 and 7 switch from the sociopolitical values placed on the growth of GNP to the evolving attention being given to inequality—that is, how total wealth is distributed throughout society, as well recent attempts to understand and explain inequality. Based on these analyses, Chap. 8 asks whether the past is a reliable prologue for understanding markets, economies, and the discipline of economics in the near future.

Before moving on, we are reminded that "social construction" seems to be a widely used concept among scholars, although it may be relatively new to economics. Sociologists use such terms as "symbolic environments," arguing that we relate to one another through the filter of language. We live in a world surrounded by symbols.[18]

The textual historian of the Christian bible, Bart Ehrman, authored a number of books on how the foundation resource for believers was manipulated for ideological purposes over the centuries.[19] Dale Martin has also written on how ideologies were created for political and cultural reasons in the far past.[20]

Relatively little has been written on the language history and not-so-hidden values of economics and economists. Yes, there are many excellent histories of economic theories and individual economists but relatively little attention has been given to the epistemological base of the discipline.

Some economists, of course, have written on the questionable value assumptions of their colleagues. Jonathan Schlefer, for example, has written that economics "is more like political philosophy, inextricably combining theoretical and moral dimensions…Political thinking cannot usefully be distilled into a pure timeless theory—and the same is true for economic thinking."[21] This should remind us that Adam Smith's *natural liberty* is a value-based "moral impulse" still accepted by many economists (and noneconomists as well). The history of economics, according to Schlefer, is "a living museum of ideas, challenges to those ideas, and responses to the challenges."

Even without the intrusions of values, economists (as well as other scientists) must make assumptions in order to better understand their world—which for economists often means assumptions about markets:

> They make simplified assumptions about the economic world we inhabit and construct imaginary economies—in other words, models—based on these assumptions. They use these imaginary economies to draw practical conclusions about the actual economies we inhabit…[but] nobody has ever seen supply or demand curves; they are models. They can be useful, but should not be mistaken for a literal picture of reality.[22]

In his *Austerity, The Great Failure*, Florian Schui comes closer to the social construction perspective found in other social sciences. He places his intellectual history of "austerity" in the centuries-old critique of consumption. "The current controversy about austerity policies is therefore ultimately about the question of whether or not rewards can be expected for abstaining from consumption." For consumption "[i]s as much a moral, religious or political and even an aesthetic question as it is an economic one."[23]

Schui explores the question of "how much consumption is right" from an historical perspective of how the general idea was understood and evaluated over the centuries—including its importance in the Keynesian bookkeeping formula for national income (consumption plus savings plus investment). While recognizing the central role that consumption plays in markets, Veblen argued that conspicuous consumption dealt with social vanity that went well beyond essential material well-being. Adam Smith seems to have agreed: those who tended to be more concerned with "elegance of…dress," "equipage," and "household furniture" gave ornament more importance than profit.[24]

Early Christian writers were not favorable to consumption, a key component of modern economics. That began to change with the Enlightenment when the public was invited "to celebrate economic growth and stop worrying about moral consequences."[25] Christ's Sermon on the Mount still remained an anchor on old thinking: No one can serve two masters. You cannot serve God and wealth. There was God on the one hand and "Mammon"—a word that denotes wealth and possessions—on the other. Yet, as we will see in later chapters, rational economic man would normatively and instinctively seek to add to his own personal wealth, and adding to the wealth of a nation was Adam Smith's policy mandate.

Martin Luther, according to Schui, let Protestants off the hook of Christian morality by claiming that the bible's lessons applied only to the spiritual, not to worldly laws, values, and norms. The "spiritual commitment to poverty did not translate into a challenge to the property rights of the rich in the temporal world."[26] The moral stigma of accumulating wealth was lifted.

This brief historical review of economics and economists suggests that "even professional economists are just as much slaves of centuries-old moral and religious teachings."[27]

Just as Christian followers changed their founding religious texts, according to Ehrman, economists and others redefined mankind over time. Mankind to economists means "economic man," an Enlightenment concept that we will revisit in later chapters.

According to Schui, "classical economics still operated with assumptions about economic behavior that were often utopian. Smith, like all self-respecting thinkers of the Enlightenment, expected individuals to behave rationally."[28] Institutions were created over time to impose this ideology on society.

In addition to rationality, accumulating "wealth" was the assumed value that societies should strive to create. Not all economists, of course, held this same value. Keynes, for example, suggested another amorphous concept: "'The love of money' could never be a goal in itself. Wealth was only a means not an end." Keynes substituted the squishy concept of a "good life," the kind he was personally able to enjoy.[29]

Modern economics rests on a sandbar of values with shifting social objectives, basic units of markets and economies, and assumed selfish and other forces that drive and give shape to markets over time. These assumed forces and units presumably help explain and then justify why some of us are wealthier than others. There is nothing providential in the way society works or where you fit into it. Morality is irrelevant—unless many of our basic assumptions are built on questionable value judgments.

"Inequality" is one of the value and factual topics currently de jure in economics. Thomas Piketty,[30] Anthony Atkinson,[31] Joseph Stiglitz,[32] Angus Deaton,[33] and Monica Prasad,[34] among others, have recently explored the origins and consequences of inequality, a "sponge term" requiring a cleansing of moral overtones.[35] This is one of the epistemological and empirical challenges of our recent time. It also provides us a window into understanding some of the not-so-hidden assumptions made by economists. We will see that the term "inequality" has both descriptive (factual) and moral meanings. We will not cover the literature that addresses the possible influences on patterns of inequality. Piketty is a good source for this literature.

Instead of economists' monograph on economics, the present book places the concept of inequality within the larger epistemological tradition of this social science discipline. In doing this, we will hopefully appreciate that inequality is just one of no doubt legions of other morally tinged words in the dictionaries of economists. Chapter 5, for example, explores some of the value judgments that are used to measure national income and product (wealth).

So what follows is not your traditional economics text, nor is it a standard history of economic theory, one that identifies the forces that drive markets and economies. My *A Concise History of Economists' Assumptions About Markets* is more in that tradition. Instead, the focus is more on how the values that economists themselves held helped shape how they and we today understand (and misunderstand) our modern life. The respected discipline of economics still wears the mantle of its original moral science beginnings.

So let us move on in this journey of rediscovery.

Notes

1. From General Douglas MacArthur's farewell speech to congress on April 19, 1951.
2. I am not aware of studies of how economists are socialized into the inner temples, scriptures, and hierarchy of saints and sinners within their most holy discipline. Robert Merton, George Reader, and Patricia Kendall edited a series of studies on the many changes experienced by medical students on their way through their training to the final "white coat ceremony" admitting them as licensed physicians. See their *The Student-Physician: Introductory Studies in the Sociology of Medical Education* (Harvard, 1957). Columbia University's Wagner Thielens, Jr.'s PhD dissertation adopted the same panel study method for his multiyear longitudinal tracking of students passing through that university's school of law. There are many studies of the languages that the different disciplines require of their members. E.g., Paul F. Lazarsfeld and Raymond Boudon, *On Social Research and Its Language* (Chicago, 1993). I suspect that most graduate students in economics had undergraduate majors in economics (and/or math), suggesting that the socialization process began before entering the final sorting-out graduate school years.
3. Chris Beneke, "The Myth of American Religious Coercion," www.common-place.org vol. 15 no. 3 Spring 2015.
4. The author has done his best to avoid using analogies, a danger well explained by David Hackett Fischer in his *Historians' Fallacies: Toward a Logic of Historical Thought* (New York: Harper & Row, 1970). Economists themselves seem less inclined to soften their criticisms of false prophets and their errant bibles. The following chapters reference some of the economists who have peddled their own theologies. For other references, see my *A Concise History of Economists' Assumptions About Markets: From Adam Smith to Joseph Schumpeter* (Praeger 2014).
5. From his 1930 book *The Bramble Bush, The Classic Lectures on the Law and Law School.*

6. Yes, "peddling," as in the title of Paul Krugman's *Peddling Prosperity* (Norton, 1994).
7. John Gray, *The Soul of the Marionette: A Short Inquiry into Human Freedom* (Farrar, Straus and Giroux), 2015.
8. I also noted that while there are excellent histories of economic theories as they developed in an ever-changing world, some critics charged that the "recent revival of intellectual history" recognizes that "historians of the past had carried out their work based on rather simple minded understanding of meaning and understanding." Many intellectual historians today in the tradition of the Annales School, e.g., place ideas in a larger sociocultural context to explore the diffusion, reception, production, and consumption of ideas. These historians link ideas to institutional history and the uses of ideas, not just to the history and meaning of their creation. And some of those writing in the new history framework adopt a bottom-up approach rather than what Darnton has labeled a "summit view." Contextualization is one of the new buzz concepts, a view that distinguishes not just between elites (those covered in this book) but also how the dictionaries and theories of these elites were diffused and acted upon over time by other economists, policy-makers, and different segments of the larger community.
9. Mary Poovey, University of Chicago Press, 1998.
10. Poovey, University of Chicago Press, 2008.
11. Immanuel Wallerstein, *The Limits of Nineteenth-Century Paradigms: Unthinking Social Science* (Temple, 2001, second edition).
12. This book is based on a course the author, a noneconomist, led at the Harvard Institute for Learning in Retirement.
13. Smith's chapter begins with: "THE GREAT commerce of every civilized society is that carried on between the inhabitants of the town and those of the country. It consists in the exchange of rude for manufactured produce, either immediately, or by the intervention of money, or of some sort of paper which represents money. The country supplies the town with the means of subsistence, and the materials of manufacture. The town repays this supply by sending back a part of the manufactured produce to the inhabitants of the country. The town, in which there neither is nor can be any reproduction of substances, may very properly be said to gain its whole wealth and subsistence from the country. We must not, however, upon this account, imagine that the gain of the town is the loss of the country. The gains of both are mutual and reciprocal, and the division of labour is in this, as in all other cases, advantageous to all the different persons employed in the various occupations into which it is subdivided."
14. The marginalist school of economic thought seems to have assumed that with the arrival of abundant resources, the challenge of adding wealth had been solved. See the later references to Monica Prasad's pathbreaking *A Land of Too Much* (Harvard, 2012).

15. Emphasis added to demonstrate that, yes, economists use evaluative terms.
16. Both Marshall and the decades-earlier Thomas Malthus married late in their lives. Adam Smith was a life-long bachelor, whereas Karl Marx was engaged to Jenny when he was 18. Following their marriage seven years later, the young loving couple produced seven children, one of whom died in childbirth. Marx's soft romantic heart is reflected in his 1836 or 1837 love sonnet to his wife-to-be. One of the verses read (in English translation):

    Take all, take all these songs from me,
    That Love at your feet humbly lays,
    Where, in the Lyre's full melody,
    Soul freely nears in shining rays.
    Oh! if Song's echo potent be,
    To stir to longing with sweet lays,
    To make the pulse throb passionately,
    That your proud heart sublimely sways,
    Then shall I witness from afar,
    How Victory bears you light along,
    Then shall I fight, more bold by far,
    Then shall my music soar the higher;
    Transformed, more free shall ring my song,
    And in sweet woe shall weep my Lyre.

    Marx, no more than other economists, was free of "feelings." His other feelings (e.g., regarding "oppression") helped shape his understanding of markets, how they are organized, what drives them, and who most benefits from market activities. See my *A Concise History*.
17. Later economists such as George Akerlof scoffed at the assumptions necessary to support rational exchanges and markets. His article "The Market for Lemons" (the theory of adverse selection) turned some economists' attention to the many ways that being imperfectly rational can create what seems to be an irrational market. But more on this later.
18. "Surrounded by Symbols" appears in the title to Hans Zetterberg's *The Many-Splendored Society: Surrounded by Symbols* (CreateSpace, 2009). Zetterberg provides a quick guide through the "Mead and Sussarian symbols," Emile Durkheim's "collective representations," and Mary Douglas' *How Institutions Think*. There is a vast micro-sociological literature on the creation and importance of symbolic worlds—e.g., Alfred Schutz's "The Phenomenology of the Social World (1932), Peter Berger and Thomas Luckmann's "The Social Construction of Reality" (1966), Herbert Blumer's "Symbolic Interactionism" (1969), and Erving Goffman's ever-popular "The Presentation of Self in Everyday Life" (1959).

19. Bart Ehrman, *How Jesus Became God: The Exaltation of a Jewish Preacher from Galilee* (Harper One, 2014). In his *Misquoting Jesus* (Harper, 2005), he covers the history of how the Christian bible was deliberately as well as without intention socially changed (constructed) over time. E.g., see his chapters 3 and 6. He extended the latter into his *How Jesus Became God.* For how ancient Judaism's history was artificially socially created, see Israel Finkelstein and Neil Asher Silberman, *The Bible Unearthed: Archaeology's New Vision of Ancient Israel and the Origin of its Sacred Texts* (Simon & Schuster, 2001).
20. Martin, Dale, *Inventing Superstition, From the Hippocratics to the Christians* (Harvard, 2004).
21. Jonathan Schlefer, *The Assumptions Economists Make* (Harvard, 2012), 31.
22. Ibid., 25.
23. Florian Schui, *Austerity, The Great Failure* (Yale, 2013), 3, 4.
24. Smith, *Wealth of Nations*, vol. 1, p. 324.
25. Ibid., 7.
26. Ibid., 28.
27. Ibid., 30.
28. Ibid., 103.
29. Ibid., 106.
30. Thomas Piketty, *Capital in the Twenty-First Century* (Belknap, 2013).
31. Anthony Atkinson, *Inequality. What Can Be Done* (Harvard, 2015).
32. Stiglitz, Joseph, *The Great Divide, Unequal Societies and What We Can Do About Them*, (Norton, 2015). In 2001, he won the Nobel Memorial Prize in Economic Sciences.
33. Angus Deaton, *The Great Escape: Health, Wealth, and the Origins of Inequality* (Princeton, 2013). The author was winner of the 2015 Nobel Memorial Prize in Economic Sciences.
34. Monica Prasad, *A Land of Too Much* (Harvard, 2012).
35. Inequality has attracted the attention of economists, philosophers, and ideologues, with an avalanche of books both defending and attacking inequality with little or no attention to how the very term was socially created. Some of the more recent books on inequality include William Watson, *The Inequality Trap: Fighting Capitalism Instead of Poverty* (University of Toronto, 2015); Harry G. Frankfurt, *On Inequality* (Princeton, 2015); Matthew P. Drennan, *Income Inequality: Why It Matters and Why Most Economists Didn't Notice* (Yale, 2015); Clement Fatovic, *America's Founding and the Struggle Over Economic Inequality* (University Press of Kansas, 2015); and Christopher G. Faricy, *Welfare for the Wealthy: Parties, Social Spending, and Inequality in the United States* (Cambridge University, 2015).

CHAPTER 2

The Trajectory of the First Social Science

Abstract Most histories begin with the beginning. This chapter starts at the end with an overview of contemporary subspecialties, claims about the purpose of economics, ideological camps, and different guiding principles. There are multiple socially constructed Alice-in-Wonderland mental models of economies.

If some historians are correct in criticizing the use of modern economic thinking as a way to understand premodern economies, is it also possible that some of our contemporary economic vocabularies and mental models blind economists from understanding today's ever-changing markets? Economists are not exempt from historical fallacies.

This chapter ends with the question to be pursued later: if all economists use the same economics-speak, facts, and numbers, why are there differences in how inequality is understood and explained?

Keywords Ideology • Fallacy • Markets • Guiding principles • Premodern • Economics-speak • Vocabulary

Economists are not exempt from the criticisms that philosophers have made of historical fallacies. Some (certainly not all) of Adam Smith's "old think" may be ready for the garbage bin of history.

© The Editor(s) (if applicable) and the Author(s) 2016

R.E. Mitchell, *The Language of Economics*,
DOI 10.1007/978-3-319-33981-8_2

Economists, however, can proudly claim to be the first academic social science to break free of moral philosophy, although later chapters will identify the long lives of key value-based assumptions.

The discipline has made many major contributions over its fairly long history since Adam Smith published his pathbreaking *An Inquiry into the Nature and Causes of the Wealth of Nations* in 1776. Over the past two-plus centuries, the population of trained economists has grown and is now one of the most popular undergraduate majors in many universities and colleges.

Rather than begin this history with Adam Smith, we start at the other end: today's population of economists, their publishing outlets, their diversification into multiple subspecialties, and the appearance of competing value-based schools of thought.

Once this background is in place, we will be able to better identify some of the value assumptions and contrasting rationales that have had a long life within the discipline. The following chapters further explore the moral and value dimension of the history of economics and where the discipline stands on certain issues today.

Central to this intellectual history are two streams of criticisms leveled against the central role that some economists have given to "rationality" and "rational economic man." Some of the criticisms raised by behavioral economists are covered in the following chapter, whereas Chap. 4 places "rationality" in the larger context of Enlightenment philosophers' search for the basis of order in a society rapidly transitioning toward what we now experience as a highly commercial economy. "Old think" needed to be replaced by an understanding based on the real world of the day.

What and Why Economists Do What They Do

According to Lionel Robbins, economics is a science of "rational behavior." The American Economic Association defines the discipline as "the study of how people choose to use resources," while Noble Prize–winning Paul Samuelson defined his discipline as the "study of how societies use scarce resources to produce valuable commodities and distribute them among different people." Adam Smith saw his field as "an enquiry into the nature and causes of the wealth of nations." Except for Robbins, "rationality" is not necessarily central to an understanding of markets and economies. Many economists, however, still seem to agree with Robbins.

We will return frequently to the implications that flow from Smith's definition.

According to Paul Krugman, "we actually know quite a lot about economics—more than we know in any other social science—because economics studies human beings in their simplest (if least edifying) activities. The marketplace is special among social interactions in that it is subject to certain logical regularities."[1] Yes, "logical"!

Textbooks on economics often provide their own definitions of what economics is and what economists do. In his insightful *The Worldly Philosophers: The Lives, Times and Ideas of the Great Economic Thinkers*, Robert Heilbroner wrote: "Economics [is] an explanation system whose purpose is to enlighten us to the workings, and therefore to the problems and prospects, of that complex entity we call the economy." He also wrote that "this search for order and meaning of social history…lies at the heart of economics." Alfred Marshall had a somewhat analogous definition (among his several) in his term "organan" (some spell it organon), "an engine," according to Sylvia Nasar in her *Grand Pursuit: The Story of Economic Genius*, useful for discovering truth but not a body of truth itself," "an apparatus of the mind."[2]

The Discipline's Numerical Expansion and Diversification

In my *Concise History*, I provide numbers on the growth and diversification of the discipline during the recent past. For example, the *Journal of Economic Literature*'s classification system expanded from 10 general economic and 45 subcategories in 1969, the first year the Nobel Prize in Economics was awarded, to 21 general economic categories and 132 subcategories in 2010. The average number of journals publishing the work of economists expanded from 214 for the period 1970–1979 to 824 journals for the years 2000–2007.

These quantities only refer to relatively recent decades, whereas the birth of economics, as already noted, is often dated to at least 1776, the year Adam Smith published his *The Wealth of Nations.*

Economists are not shy in pigeon-holing their colleagues into such categories as classical revival, history and institutions, the Chicago School of micro economics, free market economics, game geeks, general equilibrium, behaviorists, stock market casino, financial, Keynesians, conceptual, experimental, mainline, mainstream, Freshwater, Saltwater, and so on and on. These terms suggest that the limited mental models to be summarized later do not capture the full diversity found among contemporary economists. However, most, if not nearly all, economists incorporate in their thinking the vocabulary invented by the founders of modern economics, including Adam Smith with his economic man, the invisible hand, and the division of labor.

Ideological Camps Based on Competing Value Assumptions

Not all economists came out of the same mold either in the past or in recent time. In his *Peddling Prosperity,* Paul Krugman takes pain to distinguish between more academically neutral economists and the growing population of think tank–based public-policy ideologues and talking heads who represent different positions along the political and value spectrum.

In my *A Concise* History, I reference one well-recognized distinction between Freshwater and Saltwater schools of thought (and value assumptions):

> Freshwater economists seem to assume that economic men act rationally and as a result markets are rational—unless governments mess up the markets. The Saltwater opponents argue against building economic mental models based on the misconception of rational economic men who by acting rationally create rational markets that because they are rational are also efficient growth machines.

Keynes, according to Paul Krugman,[3] gave the essence of the distinction between the two orientations. Freshwater economists imply that some markets were, in Keynes' words, like "those newspaper competitions in which the competitors have to pick out the six prettiest faces from a hundred photographs, the prize being awarded to the competitor whose choice most nearly corresponds to the average preferences of the competitors as a whole; so that each competitor has to pick, not those faces which he himself finds prettiest, but those that he thinks likeliest to catch the fancy of the other competitors."[4]

Such markets, according to Keynes, consist of speculators who chase the guesses of their competitors, a practice that is not the best way for markets and economies to have their business decisions made and wealth added to the nation. "When the capital development of a country becomes a by-product of the activities of a casino, the job is likely to be ill-done."

Economists openly recognize and discuss these intradiscipline differences, including the contrasting theories of two economists who shared the same 2013 Nobel Prize in economics: Eugene Fama and Robert Shiller. Shiller argued that efficient markets are a myth, and that market moves very frequently do not correspond with investors' best interests.[5] He also "suggested his fellow laureate must feel like a Catholic priest who has discovered God does not exist."[6] Economists can be sharp-tongued.

Well-funded advocacy centers promote competing ideological myths and supposed truths about markets and the values on which they are assumed to be based. The so-called Adam Smith free-market Cato Institute based on Friedrich von Hayek's idea of free markets and individual liberty is one such center that has hired-hand ideologues, including some of who were trained in economics. (It was originally founded in 1974 as the Charles Koch Foundation.) The Heritage Foundation, another equally ideological think tank, was created by various right-wing supporters. It is based in Washington, DC, with a stated mission to "formulate and promote conservative public policies based on the principles of free enterprise, limited government, individual freedom, traditional American values, and a strong national defense." No mention is made of a search for truth and understanding. Instead, the intention is to confirm if not manufacture a path from the bad past to the Alice-in-Wonderland perfect future.

Instead of relying on a limited number of wealthy sponsors promoting and protecting the very status that Adam Smith criticized (as we reference elsewhere), the conservative American Enterprise Institute for Public Policy Research created in 1943 relies on grants and contributions from a wider audience "to defend the principles and improve the institutions of American freedom and democratic capitalism, limited government, private enterprise, individual liberty and responsibility, vigilant and effective defense and foreign policies, political accountability, and open debate." These centers often seem to have answers in search of questions.

There are also independent and more centrist (nonpartisan)-leaning policy centers with a heavy economic orientation. These include the Brookings Institution (1916), the National Bureau of Economic Research (1920), and the RAND Corporation (1943) among many others. Both the federal and state governments have created their own centers, and such centers exist throughout academic departments of economics in America and elsewhere. Few of these, however, can match the conservative centers in their ideologically driven paid-for political lobbying power.[7]

Many economists, of course, are clearly aware that their discipline is distorted by not-so-hidden value assumptions. John Maynard Keynes, for example, wrote:

> Let us clear from the ground the metaphysical or general principles upon which, from time to time, laissez-faire has been founded. It is not true that individuals possess a prescriptive "natural liberty" in their economic activities. There is no "compact" conferring perpetual rights on those who Have or on those who Acquire. The world is not so governed from above that private and social interest always coincide. It is not so managed here below that in practice they coincide. It is not a correct deduction from the principles of economics that enlightened self-interest always operates in the public interest. Nor is it true that self-interest generally is enlightened; more often individuals acting separately to promote their own ends are too ignorant or too weak to attain even these. Experience does not show that individuals, when they make up a social unit, are always less clear-sighted than when they act separately.[8]

Adam Smith himself recognized that the real world was strikingly different from the value-based nirvana that he thought would be best for all citizens:

> People of the same trade seldom meet together, even for merriment and diversion, but the conversation ends in a conspiracy against the public, or in some contrivance to raise prices...Civil government, so far as it is instituted for the security of property, is in reality instituted for the defence of the rich against the poor, or of those who have some property against those who have none at all.[9]

Despite the real world that he imagined, Smith's mental model described another Alice-in-Wonderland universe, one with a never-realized ideal system that if it could somehow exist would be everyone's paradise. Of course, not all later economists have held the same view. Some imply that Adam Smith's nirvana economy would still suffer from short-, medium-, and longer-term business cycles—all unwelcome examples of wasted, inefficient, and misapplied scarce resources. And, of course, societies and states are more than just markets. How otherwise can one explain recurrent economic, social, and personal wars and conflicts? If all men are both equally rational and equally virtuous, there would be peace and harmony, at least in theory.[10]

Smith recognized that markets exist within larger systems. But his academic discipline over time abandoned moral philosophy for political economy followed by Alfred Marshall's decision to expunge the term "political" from the name of his academic department. Economics was now a standalone discipline, the king of the social, political, and policy sciences.

As we will explore more below, there are economists and others who are doing their best to drag institutions back into their profession. They recognize, along with Adam Smith, that there are conspiracies, conscious or not, "against the public." After all, Smith himself suggested that the distribution of wealth is a result of public policy or the lack of it. The ways that wealth and additions to it are distributed can influence changes in the total wealth of a nation, the end state that Adam Smith's ideal market was intended to create.

A Common Language If Not Common Assumptions and Values

Despite the diversity within the discipline and its hangers-on, the entire field seems wedded to a fairly common language, one that was socially constructed over the past several centuries. Members of different tribes can talk and dispute with one another because they share a common tongue. Although some components of their mental models (what Thomas Kuhn categorized as "paradigms") may differ, the inmates of contending prisons of market models talk a common socially constructed language that seems to be able to incorporate often competing ethical and social values.

Vocabularies, assumptions, and meanings have, yes, evolved over time. The real world has certainly not been ignored.

But here's the crunch: if all economists use the same economics-speak, facts, and numbers, why do economists differ in how they understand and explain inequality and other market-related challenges? Is it possible that there is little consensus on underlying facts, evidence, numbers, and the basic language tools positioned within the mental tool box of economics?

The present chapter tags some of the challenges posed by values, language, and mental models. The following chapters will build on this foundation and begin to give greater specificity to the terms that have been added over the decades to the vocabularies invented by economists. But before moving on to this explanatory challenge, a few additional necessary battle flags will be raised.

Further Background and Prologue

Yes, Adam Smith certainly recognized that the world lacked a vocabulary to understand an economy moving from agriculture to more active commerce and industry. He had to create and formalize a new one. During his early years, the strength and international stature of a country was typically thought to depend on that country's holdings of precious metals used to lubricate cross-border mercantile transactions. These treasures were the legitimate (social, value and political are different spheres) to measure the well-being of a nation. Smith had to invent a new vocabulary that better reflected the rapid commercialization and socioeconomic transformation of England. Wealth was more than an inventory of precious metals.

The language he invented was seen as an improved key to understanding England in the mid-1700s. Again, however, questions must be raised regarding assumptions, language, and basic principles adopted by the evolving field of economics. For example, Boldizzoni argued that *The Wealth of Nations* dictionary may have limited utility in understanding earlier economies. Moreover, economic and intellectual historians make a fundamental error when they rely on our contemporary "subjective" and anecdotal evidence and concepts (mental models) to understand earlier markets and economies (the fallacy of presentism).[11] But Adam Smith, the founder of modern economics, did just that by making questionable assumptions about the interests of economic man and the mysterious forces that assured the positive outcomes of men acting in their own selfish interests.[12]

Of course, neither the world nor its economies have been entirely static over time, so Smith's invented dictionary required constant updating. This continues today but with a significant caveat, as already noted: old socially constructed vocabularies, like old soldiers, never seem to fade away. Such value-biased terms as the invisible hand, laissez-faire, wealth of a nation, natural liberty, economic man, and many other word combinations are largely unquestioned truths held by many economists and others. They can easily become mental prisons consisting of conjectures, facts, numerical evidence, hypotheses, and modes of analysis that when arranged in a single package are what Thomas Kuhn labeled "normal science"—what university students learn in introductory Econ 101. But normal need not be correct.

Yes, there are many economists who question their discipline's invented vocabularies and the analyses based on them. For example,

Jonathan Schlefer's *The Assumptions Economists Make*[13] provides an insider's perspective on some of the epistemological challenges of the discipline. Dani Rodrik also explores some of his discipline's biases in his *Economics Rules: The Rights and Wrongs of the Dismal Science.*[14] And the historian David Hackett Fischer's *Historians' Fallacies: Toward a Logic of Historical Thought*[15] is a trenchant reminder of the errors that all social analysts, including economists and the present noneconomist author, can too often make. On the other hand, some economists seem reluctant to accept Heraclitus' observation that "no man ever steps in the same river twice, for it's not the same river and he's not the same man." The markets of Adam Smith's time are certainly not the same as the markets of the present.

Fischer could have had Heraclitus in mind in his discussion of "presentism." The *fallacy of presentism* or more precisely the "fallacy of *nunc pro func*," according to Fischer, involves using current events and ideas to interpret the past world that was totally different. According to the Merriam-Webster dictionary, presentism is "an attitude toward the past dominated by present-day attitudes and experiences." Some British historians viewed history from the lens of popular Whig beliefs, making the past understandable as relevant to the present, not to its own time.

Some American ideological think tanks seem to suffer from whiggishness.

Instead of asking the epistemological question of how do we know what we know, we rush in with an inherited catechism that directs us to the most important concepts, evidence, and facts that help us analyze and interpret numbers and what they, the facts and numbers, tell us about markets and economies. If everyone agreed on the same facts (evidence) and the same approach to reasoning, then there should be a consensus among economists on what the evidence means. A general theory of knowledge would suggest that. But we sense that not all economists sing from the same dictionaries.

Economics, as suggested, is divided into different (warring?) factions on what evidence is most important and what that evidence means.[16] Meaning involves tracing knowledge claims that are embedded in different "rarified social vocabularies" used to construct mental models of markets, economies, and the forces that drive them.[17] Meanings are also based on the interpretations of "facts" and "numbers," as will be explored in later chapters.

That is, economics and the other social sciences are not simple name games based on conjectures. Facts, numbers, correlations, regressions, and large computer models have moved the discipline well beyond hypotheticals and conjectures. Both the public and private sectors contribute to this movement by generating "facts, figures, and interpretations" on current economies and trends in them. By contrast, Adam Smith's generation had to rely on ersatz anecdotal information. Yes, Smith did reference numbers but he recognized their limitations.

As many authors have noted, David Ricardo "invented" the numbers he employed to explain the value of cross-border trade. Thomas Malthus compensated for the absence of statistics in England by traveling to Scandinavia for evidence (facts) to support his socially constructed mental model that contradicted Adam Smith's assumptions about the never-ending process of national improvement through market-based additions to the wealth of an artificial (socially created) unit called a "nation." There would never be sufficient food to feed a steadily increasing number of hungry mouths, according to Malthus. Happiness was a chimerical concept. (See other references to the recent publications by Angus Deaton.)

Noneconomists as well as many economists today have also questioned the centrality that policy gurus assign to aggregate national wealth. Instead of emphasizing increases in national wealth, others have turned their attention to how wealth is distributed, as we will do when we consider "inequality," whatever that word means.

Inequality is not a natural product of Adam Smith's mental model of an economy driven by rational selfish economic men whose trucking and trading is coordinated by the never-seen invisible hand, a social construct that still seems to hold sway among economists. But according to some economists and others, inequality (how the wealth of a nation is distributed) is a product of public policy, whether deliberately formulated or not. Moreover, trucking and trading bread for shoes fails to reflect some of the major changes in what drive modern societies. For example, Alex Pentland, in his *Social Physics*,[18] proposed an entirely new social network–based paradigm as the most appropriate mental model for understanding not just modern economies but also the larger social and political systems in which they operate.

Social physics will be revisited in a later chapter.

In summary, the wordsmith Adam Smith's *The Wealth of Nations* represents a pivotal point in how economists described and understood economies both in the eighteenth and in the twenty-first century. He created a new value-based mental model, a social construct populated by a vocabulary that is still much spoken today.

Economies and the world in which they are sited have continued to evolve since Adam Smith's time, but the old think seems to have a lock on many of our contemporary economists. Perhaps too few of them have heeded Socrates' advice that the unexamined life (including unexamined markets and economies) is not worth living.

Yes, as noted above, there certainly are warring camps within the discipline, but again, the members of competing tribes speak the same language; they share many of the same socially constructed meanings that include those that Adam Smith invented in the 1770s. Vocabularies, assumptions, and meanings have, yes, evolved over time. The real world has certainly not been overlooked.

But again: if all economists use the same economics-speak, facts and numbers, why are there differences in how inequality is understood and explained?

Read on.

Notes

1. Paul Krugman, *Peddling Prosperity*, xii. Some economists, critics might argue, overlook the extramarket forces that help shape these regularities. Also, as will be suggested later, "regularities" do not necessarily imply what is possible or ideal. It is important to distinguish among the present, the possible, and the ideal.
2. Sylvia Nasar, *Grand Pursuit: The Story of Economic Genius* (Simon & Schuster, 2011). Organon is a Greek word meaning "instrument, tool, organ" and is the standard collection of Aristotle's six works on logic. In 1620, Roger Bacon attacked this Aristotelian perspective in his *Novum Organum* ("The New *Organon*"). Alfred Marshall used the same term for "tool," an "engine of analysis" useful for discovering truths. He considered economics to be *a mode of enquiry* in a limited study of man. But the truths that economics could pursue were limited to the "subjective forces" connected to the pursuit of the material requisites of well-being.
3. Paul Krugman, "How Did Economists Get It So Wrong?" *New York Times Magazine* (September 2, 2009). He referred to "a 1997 publication by Andrei Schlefer of Harvard and Robert Vishny of Chicago, which amounted to a formalization of the old line that 'the market can stay irrational longer than you can stay solvent'."
4. From Chapter 12 (The State of Long-Term Investment) in his *The General Theory of Employment, Interest and Money*.

5. Rob Wile, "Robert Shiller Debunks Eugene Fama's Ideas To His Face During This Nobel Prize Presentation" available online at http://www.businessinsider.com/robert-shiller-nobel-presentation-2013-12?op=1#ixzz3fFoJD4oV.
6. Katie Allen, "Nobel prize-winning economists take disagreement to whole new level" in *The Guardian* (December 10, 2013).
7. Paul Krugman, in his *Peddling Prosperity*, distinguished between these talking-head ideologues and those with a more even-handed academic mind-set. Both sets, however, will be seen in later chapters to be captives of their respective socially constructed concepts and words.
8. From "The end of laissez-faire," an essay published as a pamphlet by the Hogarth Press in July 1926.
9. *An Inquiry into the Nature and Causes of the Wealth of Nations*, PART II: Inequalities Occasioned by the Policy of Europe.
10. Macro theories require leaps of faith about economic men: they would have similar utilities, ordered preferences, and a solid grasp of the probability that their actions would have their intended consequences. Behavioral and other economists, as we will see later, have shown that these are false assumptions.
11. Francesco Boldizzoni, *The Poverty of Clio, Resurrecting Economic History* (Princeton University Press, 2011).
12. Karl Polanyi, in his *The Great Transformation: The Political and Economic Origins of Our Time* (Beacon, 1957, but first copyrighted in 1944), took a sometimes essayist's critical approach to unmasking the hidden assumptions of economists along the same line used by Boldizzoni. Polyani's "substantiveness" explored how humans making a living interacted with their social and natural environments.
13. Jonathan Schlefer, *The Assumptions Economists Make* (Cambridge: Harvard University Press, 2102).
14. Dani Rodrik, *Economics Rules: The Rights and Wrongs of the Dismal Science* (Norton, 2015).
15. Harper & Row, 1970.
16. Economists, of course, can hold contrary views on the same topic, and they cannot but be aware of how different schools of thought interpret the same evidence and challenges. That is what was probably behind President Truman's appeal for a one-armed economist who would not tell him "On the one hand, this" and "On the other hand, that." He also said that "any man who has had the job I've had and didn't have a sense of humor wouldn't still be here." All the economists I have personally known had a good sense of humor. But as already suggested, there are differences between camps of economists regarding the empirical status of rational economic man and rational markets as conceived by Adam Smith and others. We will come back later to this difference.

17. Scholars have invented a number of terms to describe their discovery and use of invented words—e.g., *mentalité*, episteme, paradigm, hermeneutics, semiotics, hegemony, deconstruction, and thick description. According to one source, "By 1980, the history of ideas was already passé." See Darrin M. McMahon and Samuel Moyn, eds., *Rethinking Modern European Intellectual History* (Oxford, 2014), 16. Yes, this verdict obviously raises questions about what you are currently reading. Elsewhere in this same edited volume is the statement: "All of what historians knew as 'modern knowledge,' then, had been complicit in creating the microphysics of modern power and the 'iron cages' of modern institutional life." 138. These new experts on language and its uses suggest that economists' use of language is a modern form of power. Of course, that indictment is not specific to any individual discipline, but it does remind us that the iron cage of economists' vocabularies can mask some truths that protect the self-interests of certain members of market economies. Conflicting Protestant theologies brought this distinction into the public domain with contrary views between those accepting the social gospel and those, who like Billy Graham, focused on getting the individual believer "right." Whatever their theological and social beliefs, Protestant ministers in all the major denominations have a similar response to economic incentives in their own personal careers. See the author's much-dated "Polity, Church Attractiveness, and Ministers' Careers: An Eight Denomination Study of Inter-Church Mobility," *Journal for the Scientific Study of Religion* (Spring, 1966). For how denominations and churches participate in and respond to market forces, see Rodney Stark and Roger Finke, *The Churching of America 1776–2005: Winners and Losers in Our Religious Economy* (Rutgers University Press, 2005).
18. Penguin, 2014.

CHAPTER 3

An Overview of Socially Constructed Mental Models and Vocabularies

Abstract Paradigms help us make sense of the world. They are also modes of social control. Questions are raised about several basic units and assumptions held by economists—such as economic man and the invisible hand. Both concepts have been well-scrutinized in the recent past. They seem to be shaky, socially created units on which to build theories about markets.

Perhaps, economic man is a fraud. At least this seems to be the conclusion of some behavioral economists. This suggests the need for alternative evidence-based mental constructs and mental models.

Keywords Virtue • Evidence-based • Concepts • Categories • Facts • Units • Numbers • Economic man • Assumptions • Theories • Behavioral economics • Social control • Economic man • Mental model

The What and Why of Mental Models

This chapter briefly summarizes some of what we know about mental models (Kuhn's paradigms) and the socially constructed vocabularies that shape how economists and others organize the ways they view and understand markets and economies.

© The Editor(s) (if applicable) and the Author(s) 2016

R.E. Mitchell, *The Language of Economics*,
DOI 10.1007/978-3-319-33981-8_3

Kuhn popularized the term (concept) of paradigm and paradigm shift in his influential 1962 book *The Structure of Scientific Revolutions.*[1] He responded to early criticisms of his theories with a 1969 postscript to the second edition of this now classic on how language-based models influence how scientists think and what they do.

Despite the criticisms leveled against *paradigms*, the general orientations that the concept suggests seem to be fairly widely accepted, for, as Erving Goffman explained, "[w]e frame reality in order to negotiate it, manage it, comprehend it, and choose appropriate repertories of cognition and actions."

The theologian Reza Aslan makes the same claim:

> [N]o evangelist in any of the world's great religions would have been at all concerned with recording his or her objective observations of historical events. They would not have been recording observations at all! Rather they were *interpreting* those events in order to give structure and meaning to the myths and rituals of their community, providing future generations with a common identity, a common aspiration, a common *story.* After all, religion is, by definition, interpretation; and by definition, all interpretations are valid.[2]

Paradigms, or whatever one wishes to label them, help us to make sense of the world.

The term and concept, despite criticisms leveled against Kuhn's original formulation, seem widely accepted today. For example, the polyglot walking encyclopedia Immanuel Wallerstein titled one of his books *The Limits of Nineteenth-Century Paradigms: Unthinking Social Science.*[3] He covers some of the rhetorical battles fought in the fairly recent past (and certainly continue today) concerning ways to explain change through the use of testable hypotheses and the evidence they require. Inherent in some of these paradigms are meanings attached to "development" (aka Adam Smith's changes in the wealth of a nation) and assumptions about what is normal (a normative assertion), what progress means, and what explains gaps between those with more or less wealth.

Wallerstein is not alone in arguing that these paradigms are "*modes of social control,*" not just mental constructs needed to make sense of the world. At least they are blinkers that narrow the focus of economists. But they can also easily become dictionary-poor, and as a consequence, economists are locked into the past, while real markets and economies, as well as the larger systems in which they exist, move on.

Markets and economies are not independent of the larger social, cultural, and political systems in which they operate, at least that was the thinking of the older political-economy school of thought as well as later institutional economists and others.

Over time, economists have invented different catechisms, eternal truths, and orthodoxies that extend beyond narrow market operations to include actions by the state that both regulate and guarantee how markets will operate and who most or least benefits from these operations.

Wallerstein provides one of several alternatives to the predominant mental models held by contemporary economists.

Mary Poovey, among others, places the creation of these mental models and dictionaries in their detailed historical context, suggesting, perhaps, that the use of old dictionary entries can mask what is happening in the real world of today. Language and the theories based on old dictionaries can become catechisms, as they might be among some economists and especially among their talking-head allies.[4]

Why a New Economic Man Was Needed

One place to begin is with *economic man*, a mental construct of the French, Scottish, and English Enlightenments, an ideal image that replaced the less-than-noble savage of the past.

A modernizing economy needed both modern men and modern political systems (not the feudalism of the past) to assure that modern private-property-based markets would operate in ways to benefit all participants and the nation as a whole. Adam Smith postulated a selfish but rational man to fit the needs of the modernizing markets of his day.[5]

According to Lawrence Freedman, this new civilized man was strikingly different from the premodern man of biblical time:

> Many of the [biblical] stories revolve around conflicts (sometimes internecine and often with the enemies of Israel) in which trickery and deception are employed.
>
> Through the Bible we are allowed to see the factors at work that determined the history of the Israelites, but to the subjects of these stories it would have been challenging to work out what was going on. God's objectives were clear enough, but his methods were invariably deceptive, leading his victims into traps under the erroneous impression that they were masters of their destinies. As a result, deception became a strong biblical theme. *Cunning was accepted as a natural method* for an underdog who must use wits to succeed.[6]

Deception, according to Freedman, was a strong biblical theme and a natural method for the underdog to survive. Tricksters succeeded. Both Achilles and Odysseus relied on cunning (e.g., Odysseus escaped captivity by riding under a sheep). And many of us recognize Virgil's warning: "Do not trust the horse, Trojans! Whatever it is, I fear the Greeks even bearing gifts." (Laocoön in Virgil's *Aeneid*.)

Greek writers allowed noble lies for a good purpose (Plato). Centuries later, Machiavelli suggested that pure survival was the highest objective, and to be feared was better than being loved. Manipulation and deceit were accepted along with the pursuit of personal gain.

Freedman tracks these premodern satanic assumptions about how individual men related to one another over time. Moreover, man was not free, a concept that along with "individualism" would have to await later centuries to be rediscovered and redefined by such Enlightenment thinkers as Adam Smith. They had to invent a new economic man, one freed from the controls exercised by churches and religiously ordained secular leaders (monarchies and feudal lords) who maximized their own well-being at the expense of all others.

Cunning tricksters survived in ways contrary to Adam Smith's image of a modern economic man. That man, however, was not what some of Smith's near contemporaries observed in their own daily lives. For example, in his *The Complete English Tradesman* (1726, 50 years before Smith's rediscovery of this same economic actor), Daniel Defoe's truckers and traders wallowed in deceit. They were complete hypocrites so that "[a]ll the ordinary communication of life is now full of lying; and what with table-lies, salutation-lies, and trading-lies, there is no such thing as every man speaking truth with his neighbor."[7]

Defoe's tricksters had to be civilized with virtue in order for truckers and traders to trust one another. Adam Smith solved this challenge by inventing economic man. Satan, however, was always there, so punitive state action could be justified, an action that Hobbs and others earlier promoted.

Historians have traced the slow movement away from premodern man to Adam Smith's economic man. Yes, Thomas Hobbs (1588–1679) argued that the most feasible way to physically survive in a normless society and protect yourself from a nasty, brutish, and short life was by entering into a social contract with a higher-level "artificial person." Human apes had to surrender their rights to the state. This suggests that Defoe's selfish and dishonest man was not the base on which to build an ideal modern economy and society. Something else was needed.

Where did Adam Smith discover an honest virtuous economic man, the one he created in his *The Wealth of Nations*?

Perhaps, he found him among his own fellow Scotch neighbors, men of virtue who balanced selfish economic advantage with analogous selfish concern with how much honor others conferred upon oneself. But more on that later.

Let me step back in time again: a Leviathan (Hebrew for "sea monster") would protect life but not necessarily assure personal or social prosperity and additions to the wealth of a nation. Later writers such as John Locke (1634–1704) explored the kinds of society that would allow individuals within it to flourish both materially and spiritually. Attention shifted from society to its individual members. This is the intellectual atmosphere in which Adam Smith (1723–1790) and other fellow members of the Scottish Enlightenment reinvented modern man, someone who would, yes, be selfish but with a selfishness that could only be economically exercised by honest (no tricks, dishonesty nor deviousness) trucking and trading with other narrowly selfish but similarly honest truckers and traders.

Adam Smith's new truckers and traders would be mutually rewarded, for they exchanged equally valued items. The more they traded, the more they individually benefitted in a process that added to the nation's aggregate wealth while increasing their own as well. Maximizing one's own wealth maximized the wealth of all. There were no losers. All fairly contributed equally. And equal contribution and rewards were how national wealth was to be distributed among individual economic men.

Smith could not have been unaware of the devious and dishonest men of biblical and later times. To control that, Smith saw that men (or gentlemen) had a Christian civil or moral compulsion parallel to their selfish economic standing: they needed the moral respect of others. Seventeen years before his 1776 *The Wealth of Nations*, Adam Smith published his *The Theory of Moral Sentiments* (1759), a social-psychological treatise suggesting that one's social network could control one's biblical atavistic tendencies. One had to be aware of how others viewed you, for your ability to truck and trade depended on the trust others had in you. New economies and markets called forth a socially constructed post-biblical trucker and trader. Biblical man was finally unheathenized.

Economic Man Donned a Hat of Virtue

Gertrude Himmelfarb, among others, argued that

> whereas the essence of the French Enlightenment was "reason," the British Enlightenment is defined by the idea of "social virtues" that "naturally, instinctively, habitually bound people to each other" – virtues such as "respectability, responsibility, decency, industriousness, prudence and temperance."

The driving force of the British Enlightenment was not only reason but also acceptance of new "social virtues" or "social affections."[8] Leviathan was exchanged by a new population of like-minded virtuous participants in a common market.

Virtue was an essential civilizing power in all social relations, not just those specific to market transactions.

But in case virtue took a holiday, a system of laws and their enforcement was created as backup insurance.

The moral-economist Smith invented the many-sided economic man whose selfish trucking and trading was tempered by "the love of virtue… and the abhorrence of vice and injustice." The latter was essential if the atavistic biblical man was to be tamed and additions made to the wealth of a nation.[9]

Socrates saw the need for taming virtue: "[T]he more [men] think of making a fortune, the less they think of virtue."[10]

Bernard Mandeville's *Fable of the Bees*, first published in 1705, seven decades before Smith's *The Wealth of Nations*, apparently did not believe that abhorrence of vice and injustice was a requirement without which society and economies could benefit. Himmelfarb summarized Mandeville's claim that vice could lead to social virtue: "Every vice had its concomitant virtue: avarice contributed to prodigality, luxury to industry, following to ingenuity….every part was full of Vice / Yet the whole mass a Paradise."[11] Himmelfarb goes on to conclude: "A well-intentioned attempt to rid the hive of vice had the effect of ridding it of its virtues as well, resulting in the destruction of the hive itself, as all the bees, 'blest with content and honesty,' abandoned industry and took refuge in a hollow tree." (A severely backward sloping labor supply curve in the parlance of our contemporary economists.)

Smith and other members of the Scottish Enlightenment held, it seems, contrary assumptions. They saw the savage economic man tamed by virtue. Again, their mentally constructed economic man's deception and avarice (that were common in biblical and hardly absent in our own time) were tempered by a strong sense of virtue. Reason itself was not sufficient. A moral sense was essential, for how else could truckers and traders have trust in one another? Otherwise we would live in a Hobbesian world of war of all against all with no economic development nor additions to the wealth of the nation (despite Mandeville's contrary mental model).

Although the Mandeville–Smith difference has perhaps been lost over time, it is still relevant to an understanding of what kind of economic man best explains how a society can become prosperous. How important is the assumption about a virtuous rational economic man?[12]

Adam Smith and those who followed him were engineering how generations of economists and others would see and understand the world. His centuries-old eyeglasses have had a long shelf life despite fundamental changes in the real world since 1776. Our current academic departments of economics continue to make sense of the world using a now much-dated socially constructed vocabulary.[13]

Perhaps modern-day Smithians should read the Veblenish chapter Smith added to his *Theory of Moral Sentiments*: "Of the Corruption of Our Moral Sentiments, Which Is Occasioned by This Disposition to Admire the Rich and the Great, and to Despise or Neglect Persons of Poor and Mean Condition." Adam Smith was not just an economist, but as this title suggests, he was also an enlightened Scotch Presbyterian with a new understanding of natural (moral) law.

Myths Play a Role

Of course, the above is a broad generality, but it is in line with our contemporary theories (by, e.g., Erving Goffman) that "we frame reality in order to negotiate it, manage it, comprehend it, and choose appropriate repertories of cognition and action." We are taught how to think about certain issues (e.g., national wealth) to the exclusion of others (e.g., the distribution of wealth).

Moreover, as Kuhn and others have argued, claims about truth depend on structures of power. What would our contemporary economic theories be if economic man was seen to be a fraud invented during the 1700s? And if not virtuous, honest, and all-wise rational economic calculators, what would that mean for our understanding of markets and the larger systems in which they operate?

We may need the myth of economic man, the active shadow of Jesus Christ himself, the invisible behind the invisible hand! (We will see later in this chapter that, according to Milton Friedman, economists may not need rational economic men as long as the economists' formulae do an adequate job of explaining movements within an economy. Not all of Friedman's Freshwater economist colleagues would likely agree with him.) Voltaire might have been on to something when he exclaimed that "if God did not exist, one would have to invent him." And so he was. Morality to many was seen to necessarily rely on religious or religious-like foundations.[14]

Authors have been using "socially constructed" for some time with variations in how the concept is tagged. For example, some social scientists refer to "symbolic behavior as an individual's capacity to respond to or use a system of significant symbols." It has also been proposed that the reality of an organization or larger society (as well as the economy) is socially constructed through communication (language). This allows individuals to understand their environment and create a social reality. Alice in Wonderland was a socially constructed fictitious world, or so it would seem.

Relatively few economists have wandered outside the internal workings of markets and economies to consider how the social distribution of power influences the distribution of what is trucked and traded. More on that later other than to note that political power and even inequality itself are not prominent terms in the dictionaries of economists.

As we all are, Adam Smith and those who followed him were products of their time. Truckers and traders in Smith's late 1700s operated in social and economic networks much smaller and perhaps friendlier than what followed soon after 1776. This suggests that socially constructed mental models may have relatively short shelf lives.

Alex Pentland in his *Social Physics* recognized that Adam Smith created an imaginary Alice-in-Wonderland world, one much chummier than what we have today. Smith in 1776

> lived in an era where almost all the bourgeois residents in a city knew each other and were constrained by social pressure to be good citizens. Without the obligations provided by strong social ties, capitalism often turns rapacious and politics turn poisonous. In our new hyperconnected world, most ties are weak, and all too often the invisible hand no longer functions. (3)

Adam Smith largely limited trucking and trading primarily to physical goods. He did not consider services to be "productive." (So much for the virtuous readers of this paragraph!) But today's economies are heavily service-sector dominated.

Whereas economists even today may seem to accept Smith's understanding that economies are driven primarily by the trucking and trading filtered through the invisible hand, Pentland and others argue that the major drivers are filtered and distributed through social networks, not all of which are necessarily inhabited by virtuous men. In a data-driven society, "human behavior is driven by the exchange of ideas – how people cooperate to discover, select, and learn strategies and coordinate their actions – rather than how markets are driven by the exchange of money. (p. 15) Again, more on this later.[15]

A New Suit for Economic Man

We will come back later to how economists and others viewed the role that knowledge plays in markets and economies. Suffice it to note, as done above, that the social invention of a sanitized and civilized rational economic man served as a basic building block for the socially created image of a rational well-operating economy. It had to be rational because the truckers and traders within it were rational. They may not be, and no doubt were not, aware that their trucking and trading was channeled by another essential mysterious power: the invisible hand, an image also to be explored later.

Behavioral economists such as Daniel Kahneman[16] have actually studied the degree to which economic and other decisions are made on rational grounds, or at least different meanings of rationality. Instead of taking mainline economists' assumptions about how decisions should be made, he conducted research on how they are actually made.

Kahneman discovered that economic men make risky decisions without assuming anything about rationality as it is understood by economists. And utility, as conceived by economists, often revolves around what one might lose rather than what might be gained in any transaction. "Loss aversion" has an important place in the behavioral economist's toolbox.

To some investigators (e.g., Kathleen Vohs), "living in a culture that surrounds us with reminders of money may shape our attitudes in ways that we do not know about and of which we may not be proud."[17] Calculating economic man may be using a monetary yardstick to determine the relative costs and benefits of trucking and trading. And measures of national income around the world are expressed in monetary terms, a topic we will revisit later. But even personal decisions about monetary trade-offs are not made on purely (deep or extended) rational economic grounds.

Instead, Kahneman's research indicates that the decisions we make do not draw on what the reasoning implied in Adam Smith's concept of the rational calculating economic man. Instead, through a law of least effort, we tend to rely on intuitive thinking, his System 1. "Humans actually make risky choices without assuming anything about their rationality." (271) Later economists (e.g., game theorists) built other mental models based on alternative assumptions about the meaning of rationality.[18]

Kahneman discovered two different species of economic man: "the fictitious Econs, who live in the land of theory, and the Humans, who live in the real world." (p. 408)

Plausibility rather than probability characterizes System 1 thinking. (159) In contrast, System 2 thinking requires more conscious (and more time-consuming) logic rather than intuition. (165) Even then, decision-makers differ on the major criteria they use: some emphasize losses, whereas other focus on gains (risk aversion vs. risk-seeking).

According to Kahneman, "[t]he concept of loss aversion is certainly the most significant contribution of psychology to behavioral economics." (300) It is not adding to one's wealth and the wealth of the nation that is central to market decisions. Instead, it is a concern over losing wealth, a formula that could lead to stagnation and loss rather than adding to the nation's wealth.

That is, Kahneman and other behavioral economists describe

> two fictitious characters…two species and…two selves. The two characters were the intuitive System 1, which does the fast thinking, and the effortful and slower System 2, which does the slow thinking, monitors System 1, and maintains control as best it can within its limited resources. The two species were the fictitious Econs, who live in the land of theory, and the Humans, who act in the real world. (408)

Adam Smith's economic man was assumed to be a serious calculator, a System 2 man. That is what allowed the invisible hand tempered by concerns for one's self-esteem (vanity) in perfectly free markets to successfully reward all citizens while adding to the total wealth of all. If the behavioral economists' findings and claims have merit, then economists who adhere to Adam Smith's socially constructed economic man live in an Alice-in-Wonderland of unfounded assumptions divorced from the real world.

This brief overview fails to do justice to the work of Kahneman, other behavioral economists, and some mainline critics who question theories based on unrealistic socially constructed vocabularies and assumptions often inherited from the non-near past.

But economists, it should be emphasized, deal more than with general terms and concepts. The discipline also has a long history of "operationally" ***marking*** and ***measuring*** key terms so that they can be numerically manipulated.

Returning to the Question: Is Rational Economic Man Really Necessary?

Before moving on to the social history of how the language of economics was created, the reader is reminded of Milton Friedman's thinking about the meaning of rationality—which was that it was predicting what people do "on average." Not all economists agree that modern economic theories must be based on the assumption that *all* economic men are rational.

Friedman argued that theories should be judged by their ability to predict events rather than by the realism of their assumptions.[19] In his *The Methodology of Positive Economics*, he agreed that although any science (including economics) should be free of value judgments, the usefulness of economics should be judged by the accuracy of its predictions. Accuracy trumped the soundness of assumptions.[20]

He wrote:

> Truly important and significant hypotheses will be found to have "assumptions" that are wildly inaccurate descriptive representations of reality, and, in general, the more significant the theory, the more unrealistic the assumptions (in this sense).
>
> Theory (or hypothesis) must be judged by its
>
> *simplicity* in being able to predict at least as much as an alternate theory, although requiring less information;
> *fruitfulness* in the precision and scope of its predictions and in its ability to generate additional research lines.

If something is irrational then the future of markets is unpredictable. Again, he argued that if the formulae and models constructed by economists "work" fairly well in their predictive power, then it is not relevant whether economic man is rational or not. What "works," however, is open to question, for averages are just that. They imply dispersion around a mean with distributions that are not necessarily bell-shaped. Standard deviations and tails cannot be ignored.

The average may have less effect on markets than economic actors well above or below the mean, especially if those in the tails of the distribution differ significantly in their influence over economic and public policies.

Just as wealth can be statistically graphed, it should, in theory, be possible to graph the distribution of influence and thereby suggest keys to how to alter the distribution of wealth, if this became a policy objective. The two dimensions overlap one another.

Of course, economists are always looking under the hood of their computer models. But there is always a danger that their mental constructs are themselves considered unquestionable facts that can be used in pursuit of normative purposes.[21]

It is no wonder that some economic predictions are off the mark, and the farther the predictions look into the future, the more likely that averages and standard deviations will change, with consequences for the immediate and longer term.[22]

That is, markets, it seems, can be seen as systems *sui generis* and independent of economic man, whether rational or not. Friedman may have been on to something, suggesting that markets have emergent properties in themselves.

Macroeconomists seem to accept this in their manipulation of national aggregates (e.g., the accounting formula $Y = C + S + I$), although these economists also seem to assume that higher-level systems are still based on individual rational economic men. That does not mean, of course, that the higher-level system (the market) distributes resources and rewards efficiently. In the real world, the tails in the distribution of income and wealth would suggest otherwise.

Notes

1. University of Chicago, 1962.
2. Reza Aslan, *No god but God. The Origins, Evolution, and Future of Islam* (Random House, 2005), xxvi–vii. In his *Meursault Investigation* (Other Press, 2015), Kamel Daoud takes the "no god" perspective: religion, for Daoud's hero, is "public transportation I never use." Who is God to give lessons? After all, "I alone pay the electric bills, I alone will be eaten by worms in the end. So get lost!"
3. Temple University Press, 2001.
4. "[t]he very first dictionary of the English language, published in 1604. It is called *A Table Alphabeticall* by William Cawdrey, and it is a very slim

book at about 130 pages. It is not at all what we would expect from today's dictionaries...When it was published in 1604, English was just coming to be seen as a prestigious language." Anne Curzan, "A Table Alphabeticall," *Michigan Today* (August 18, 2015) available online at http://michigantoday.umich.edu/a-table-alphabeticall/.

5. In his *No god but God*, Reza Aslan claims that "[i]deals such as social egalitarianism, popular sovereignty, and the pursuit and preservation of knowledge had their origins not in Christian Europe, but in the Ummah." (p. 230). That, however, does not seem to be how Ummah societies later developed, as Aslan explained. His history of Islamic thought and societies over the centuries reminds us of the role that ideologies can play in structuring social and economic organizations. The understanding of economies and the larger structures in which they operate is colored by a sheet of ideological assumptions and sand. In his *The Three Principles of the People*, Sun Yat-Sen introduced the sheet-of-sand analogy in another context.
6. Emphasis added. Freedman, 10, 20–21.
7. Poovey, *A History of the Modern Fact*, 169. Some of our own contemporary economists might argue that being evil and employing tricks does not mean that men are not rational. But that does not seem to be how Adam Smith and others understood partners who truck and trade with one another.
8. Gertrude Himmelfarb, *The Roads to Modernity, The British, French and American Enlightenments* (Vintage, 2008), x, 19.
9. Smith and his fellow Scottish moral philosophers such as Francis Hutcheson argued that modern man needed more than reason; he also needed a strong moral sense. And moral sense is not something based on self-interest, a central feature of Smith's "calculating" economic man living in a mercantile world where the accumulation of wealth was a shared driving force. "Calculating" was a partial synonym for "rational." Hobbs' Leviathan world with the assumed social contract assured that all truckers and traders would share a common sense of rational duty, at least in theory. Leviathan and follow-on Enlightenment figures civilized economic man by tempering him with social virtue. Without the social contract, Hobbs claimed that "[i]n such condition there is no place for industry, because the fruit thereof is uncertain, and consequently, not culture of the earth, no navigation, nor the use of commodities that may be imported by sea, no commodious building, no instruments of moving and removing such things as require much force, no knowledge of the face of the earth, no account of time, no arts, no letters, no society, and which is worst of all, continual fear and danger of violent death, and the life of man, solitary, poor, nasty, brutish, and short."

10. Book VIII in Plato's *Republic* includes several references to virtue. E.g., "And in proportion as riches and rich men are honoured in the State, virtue and the virtuous are dishonoured," and "They themselves care only for making money, and are as indifferent as the pauper to the cultivation of virtue."
11. Himmelfarb, 29.
12. Schui explores how Voltaire and others answered this question. Op. cit., 41 ff.
13. There certainly are exceptions—for an example at the level of an individual enterprise, see B. J. and J. H. Gilmore, *The Experience Economy: Work Is Theatre & Every Business a Stage* (Harvard Business School Press, 1999).
14. Schui, 171.
15. In my *Concise History* book's coverage of Joseph Schumpeter and his focus on innovation and innovators, I review some of the early pathbreaking studies of social networks as they were studied in voting behavior (the two-step process), cosmopolitans and locals, and the diffusion and adoption of new prescriptions by medical doctors. Sociologists at Columbia University's Bureau of Applied Social Research innovated the study of innovations—and knowledge more generally. References will be made to this research tradition in a later chapter.
16. Kahneman, *Thinking Fast and Slow* (Farrar, Straus and Giroux, 2011). There are other analyses that add to the contributions made by behavioral economists. See, e.g., George A. Akerlof and Robert J. Shiller, *Phishing for Phools, The Economics of Manipulation & Deception* (Princeton, 2015).
17. Ibid., 56.
18. See David Warsh's August 2, 2015 blog entry "A New Magnifier, Kenneth Arrow stays under the radar" at http://www.economicprincipals.com/#sthash.QBPLcuAD.dpuf.
19. He argued for this in Essays III, IV, and V in *Essays in Positive Economics.* http://www.econ.umn.edu/~schwe227/teaching.s11/files/articles/friedman-1953.pdf.
20. Milton Friedman, *Essays in Positive Economics* (Chicago, 1953).
21. Federal agencies such as the congressional budget office and the executive branch offices that measure economic trends use different models and different assumptions to give high, medium, and low projections.
22. Chaos theories argue that even minimal changes in given conditions can over time have significant effects later on.

CHAPTER 4

From Metaphor to Fact: The Early History of Creating a New Language of Markets and Economies

Abstract Economists invent make-believe markets based on questionable assumptions. Over time, categories were defined. Facts to represent the categories were created and then converted to numbers so that they could be mathematically manipulated. This chapter asks: What is a fact about markets and economies? How does one move from metaphor and conjecture to fact? What value and moral assumptions impinge on economic images and facts? What is wealth? Why does it play such a central role in economics? What are the units and measures of wealth? What other units might be considered? How does the selection of basic units shape the way economists think? What is overlooked when the focus is on wealth? Who has the say on what are facts?

Keywords Mary Poovey • Metaphors • Virtue • Evidence-based • Concepts • Categories • Facts • Numbers • Economic man • Assumptions • Theories • Behavioral economics • Language • Make-believe • Invent • Dictionary • Wealth

Mary Poovey and other historians have added to our understanding of when, how, and why the early language of economics was invented. The real world of the past was not an ideal one, so early economists invented make-believe markets that, if ever allowed to exist, would be a nirvana for all. This invention required a number of questionable assumptions not

© The Editor(s) (if applicable) and the Author(s) 2016
R.E. Mitchell, *The Language of Economics*,
DOI 10.1007/978-3-319-33981-8_4

based on the facts of the time or later. The resulting mental models were fictions. But over time, economists refined their categories, arranged for facts to represent the categories, and converted the facts to numbers so that they could be mathematically manipulated.

The unknowns were operationalized in ways to mimic Adam Smith's imaginary perfect markets.

The discipline, however, is still mired in metaphors promoted by competing soothsayers. It is little wonder that critics both within and outside the discipline have commented on the limitations of economic dictionaries, theories, and fellow economists.

There are many excellent histories of economists and economic thought dating back to Adam Smith and earlier.[1] From the perspective of socially created vocabularies on their way to the science of economics, few authors can match the creative contributions that Mary Poovey made in her two earlier-referenced books. I will unashamedly draw heavily on her work. This will help remind readers that there are alternatives to the ways that our contemporary behavioral economists understand economic man.

The present chapter explores several components of the historical invention of economics and the dictionaries created to understand changes in markets.

Among the several objectives of this current chapter are tracing how metaphors, conjectures, and mental models (all socially constructed) were operationalized so that economists could work with facts and numbers. This process of operationalizing vague metaphors was not just a scientific quest parallel to what was happening in the hard sciences. It was also a search for the moral principles on which society is based, or should be based.

As we will suggest in this and in the following chapters, moral judgments (values) were made regarding economic man and the invisible hand. That is, yes, economists over the decades have contributed greatly to our understanding of market economies. At the same time, economists seem to have implanted in the public mind and in the minds of fellow economists that there is an achievable perfect market, one infused with values and populated by narrowly rational economic men.

Readers are encouraged to absorb Poovey's detailed history of how economists over time added increasing specificity to the discipline's vocabulary on the way to creating what some claim to be a useful science on how economies could (in theory) add wealth that would benefit all those who contribute to it.

The present chapter places Poovey's contributions in a somewhat broader perspective, one that considers the legacy that Adam Smith's "old think" has on present-day economics. Some of our contemporary economists, despite their many welcoming contributions, appear not to have moved very far from the assumed laws of Scotland's economy of 1776. This anchor of the past can blind one to some of the mysteries of the present.

The Ideal as a Benchmark

Adam Smith is sometimes considered the first modern economist, one who had a reasonably comprehensive and coherent view of how markets operate and what drives them (a focus of my *A Concise History*). Among Smith's many contributions is an array of abstract, often *protopsychological* metaphors that moved from the individual man (basic human nature or a single mind fully shared by all) to an awareness that men pursued different occupations organized in productive units (the division of labor) and then under an assumed but unseeable process, the invisible hand, added to everyone's personal wealth as well as the collective wealth of the nation.[2]

From these and other hypothetical basic units and processes, Adam Smith constructed an *ideal economic system*, a standard useful in assessing the deleterious influences found in the real world. Yes, he could reference examples of what his metaphors and conjectures meant—such as his use of an illustrative pin factory to explain the division of labor.[3] Other "harder" evidence is quoted in Smith's later chapters of his *Wealth of Nations*, but he apparently recognized that such evidence was probably flawed.

Along with others of his time and for decades later, economists were forced to invent their own new vocabularies without the benefit of facts that would validate their assumptions as well as relations among numbered facts.

Adam Smith lived in a world with relatively few words relevant to the markets of his time. He launched the creation of a new dictionary that would, he hoped, best capture the real world. In doing so, he was also creating a new understanding of ideal Alice-in-Wonderland economies based on economic actors' rational subjective maps, the ideal moral sentiments of his time, and how the components of his maps and markets related to one another in a highly predictable way. His mental model was a rule-based one with general laws that helped explain order in society.

Just as Isaac Newton discovered mathematical laws to explain individual particulars, Adam Smith moved toward discovering general laws that explained order in both markets and the societies in which they operated. The assumed laws and markers (evidence) required facts that could be numbered so that later economists could hypothesize what-if questions, one of the marks of a true science.

Markets energized by never-to-be seen make-believe universal economic men who fairly trucked and traded under the constraints and guidance of another unseen and unmeasurable force, an invisible hand, contributed to the increasing wealth of all. No providential design need be assumed. Markets were *sui generis*, although it was obvious that there were immoral barriers that could interfere with the operation of the hidden invisible hand. Smith was very aware of these threats to the invisible hand. There were obvious visible elbows—then and certainly so today. And, as later economists have emphasized, "Adam Smith's invisible hand—the idea that free markets lead to efficiency *as if by an invisible hand*—is invisible at least in part because it is not there."[4]

This, of course, is an oversimplified summary of the subjective macro and micro mental model that Adam Smith created and the baseline for what later economists elaborated with facts, numbers, and findings to replace conjectures and metaphors.

Poovey explored the mental building blocks Smith had to construct in moving from the unseen past to the imaginary present. Smith began to create a dictionary of economic assumptions based on his identification of

general categories,
facts to represent the categories, and
ways to count (number) the facts

so that future economists, just like Newton, could paint a portrait of the current economy, trends in it, and reasons why the real economy differed from the ideal. His teleological framework provided a standard against which current policies could be morally judged with regard to their effect on the teleological purpose of markets: to add to the wealth of the nation.

The socially constructed mental images traceable to Adam Smith and others continue to influence how our contemporaries understand and analyze markets and economies. Smith created a new science of wealth that assumed that wealth creation was the primary reason for modern man and societies.[5]

Operationalizing the Unknown

During much of the eighteenth and nineteenth centuries, England was number-poor, at least in numbers that were relevant to the markets and economies that Smith was attempting to mentally model. In exploring changes in this evidence wasteland over time, Poovey distinguished between the discovery of "facts" (empirical anchoring of metaphors) and the use of "numbers" so that larger aggregations (e.g., number of factories, currency flows, and changes in prices) could provide economists with tools to more deeply mine the mental models they initially based on metaphors. Numbered facts, of course, do not necessarily confirm that facts adequately represent all the important market components and processes that economists have invented over time.

Along with other thinkers of his day, Smith seemed to have assumed that markets and economies, if left to operate freely from private and government constraints, were always trending toward some positive state of equilibrium that continually added to the wealth of the nation and all economic men. But real-world economies were often in perpetual business cycles along with panics, bank failures, poverty, and other painful disruptions by truckers and traders. Over our own past 30 years alone, market economies have suffered more than 100 crises, some much more damaging than others.[6]

Are these normal failures inherent in modern capitalism, and if so, should economists revise the dictionaries and assumptions they use to construct their mental models of modern society? And are there alternative ways to organize society that can assure maximum liberty, wealth, and well-being? What array of goals and objectives should public policy emphasize, and how are the alternatives to be prioritized? And is there something about how we are currently organized and the vocabularies in our dictionaries that inhibit us from thinking outside the mental cubicles in which we are currently imprisoned?

Perhaps, Samuel Butler was correct: Erewhon spelled backward approximates nowhere. Did the Enlightenment fail to produce a new virtuous economic man? And is he still often absent without leave?

In her *Genres of the Credit Economy*, Poovey covers the development of a popular financial news press and the public's interest in understanding the whats and whys of the economic networks in which they lived, trucked, and traded. There were many such writers both before but especially after Adam Smith. For example, *The Economist* magazine's long history began in 1843. (It has been described as "a product of the Caledonian liberalism of Adam Smith and David Hume."[7])

A new breed of professional economist was also born. John Stewart Mill published his 1848 classic *Principles of Political Economy*, a text lasting until being replaced in 1890 by Cambridge University's Alfred Marshall's *Principles of Economics.* (Oxford University continued to use Mill's classic as a basic economics text until 1919.) According to Mill, markets were law-governed systems led by truckers and traders concerned only with accumulating personal wealth. In order to understand markets operating according to rational rules, it is necessary to understand rational economic man, the kind of person who just read this sentence.

All of the hard and softer sciences have made great strides since the late eighteenth century, the world and the society that Adam Smith and his Enlightenment contemporaries were attempting to understand with new assumptions, conjectures, and metaphors that could, over time, mimic the mathematical models of Isaac Newton and the attention given to observable evidence, predictability, and simplicity as emphasized by the Royal Society of London for Improving Natural Knowledge. Founded in 1660, the society benefitted from Newton's leadership from 1703 until his death in 1727.[8]

That is, to understand early economists is also to understand the world in which they lived.

Mary Poovey is among the many historians who have addressed this challenge. As already suggested, she identifies and questions some of the metaphors, conjectures, not-so-hidden values, and socially constructed mental models created, taught, and used by Enlightenment thinkers who had rediscovered the "individual" who exercised "free will" in the relentless pursuit of personal monetary gain (wealth).

To explore more on how economists over time visualized markets, I turn to some of the questions that Poovey successfully explored, including the contributions that Adam Smith made to the vocabularies recorded in our own contemporary economic dictionaries and the literature that uses the words so recorded.

As much belabored earlier, these words are, among other things, "epistemological units," the prisms through which we perceive and understand markets and economies. Poovey traced the historical creation of some of these key units before, during, and after Adam Smith. Either directly or through implication (at least as I understand it), she asks questions about words created to capture the meaning of what could not be seen as well as some of the moral values and other assumptions hidden in the epistemological units. Among her rephrased questions are:

> What is a fact, that is, a fact about markets and economies, not just individual economic men? And how does one move from metaphor and conjecture to fact?
>
> What if any value and moral assumptions impinge on mentally-created economic images and facts?
>
> What is wealth and why does it play such a central role in economics? What are the units and measures of wealth (e.g., prices and quantities)? What units other than wealth might be considered but not yet accepted? Why some measures rather than others? And how does the selection of basic units shape the way economists think? What is overlooked, if anything, when the focus is on wealth, its creation and its creators?
>
> Who creates what kinds of wealth? (Adam Smith did not consider service providers as wealth-creators.)
>
> Why count some facts (giving them numbers)? How are general epistemological units operationalized?
>
> How can facts be manipulated for explanatory purposes? What does explanation (not statistically-significant correlations and measures of variance) mean in economics (and the social sciences)?
>
> Who has the say on what are facts and how to understand them? Why some facts rather than others?
>
> What is a market other than economic men trucking and trading with one another?
>
> What assumptions are made about economic man—for example, are all economic men essentially the same selfish animals in pursuit of personal wealth? Is economics built on assumptions about a one-dimensional economic man striving to gain wealth and wealth only? Was Aristotle on to something in claiming that the pursuit of wealth for its own sake was endless, whereas "the art of managing a household" had natural limits, its own equilibrium?[9]
>
> Is the invisible hand an assumed essence and process? How does one operationalize invisible essences and processes including natural liberty? What explains visible fists and other aberrations found in the real world?
>
> Are economic men just puppets acting out scripts authored by an outside invisible power in a mythical market? If so, how does one explain off-script developments such as business cycles, inflation, unemployment, poverty and, yes, high degrees of inequality?

> Are scripts the same as laws. And was John Stuart Mill (1806–73) correct in claiming that an economy is a rule-governed system—or as Larry Summers claimed: "there are economic laws like there are physical laws, and as with physical laws, economic laws do not yield to political will."[10]

In a probabilistic world of science, what are the limits of painting the economy by numbers ("paint each numbered section with the colors corresponding to that number and end up with our own Starry Night that looks just like Van Gogh's!") when the world is not free of black swans or butterflies in the Amazon?[11]

I am not aware that any economists have followed the odds-giving advice proposed by Neustadt and May: "How much of your own money would you wager that the presumed thing actually happens?" And "what new *Knowns* would bring you to change items *Presumed*?"[12]

I suggest that you reread these two questions a number of times.

Creative Soothsayers

Economists bring powerful and welcome tools to the policy table, but modesty would also be welcome. "Economics-speak" has not-so-hidden value assumptions and moral judgments. In this regard, Paul Krugman's *Peddling Prosperity* provided a brief but insightful history of economist-soothsayers posing as truth-sayers, suggesting (at least to me) that the discipline has its quota of imaginative novelists and moral guardians of the invisible hand, philosophers who can stray from the path of traditional science.

One can be led easily astray when the soothsayers ably employ advanced mathematical and statistical formulae in their imaginary worlds. These and other economists as well as noneconomists are, in the words of Robert Heilbroner, as earlier noted, searching for "an explanation system whose purpose is to enlighten us to the workings, and therefore to the problems and prospects, of that complex entity we call the economy." This "search for order and meaning of social history…lies at the heart of economics."

Economists, of course, are not the only ones pursuing this same objective. Some noneconomists, as will be suggested later, may have a clearer understanding of how and why markets operate in the ways they have done in the past, why some public purposes have not been achieved or even pursued, and alternative ways to add to the wealth of a nation so that wealth is more widely shared.

Also, as noted earlier, one needs to use words (language) in the historical search process. That is one reason why applied epistemology can be helpful in discovering the discovery process adopted over the generations by economists.

Now to move from the value-laden conception of the idealized economic man to the ideal of a rational market.

We saw earlier that economists created the fictitious economic man who, with his free will, trucks and trades with multiple other free wills. But economic men are also imprisoned in a social network that went well beyond Daniel Defoe's 1719 novelistic account of the two-person exchange relationship between Robinson Crusoe and his Man Friday.[13] Adam Smith and others (especially Alfred Marshall because of his own fieldwork collecting information from individual firms) moved beyond universal economic man to ever larger collections of economic men who, although competing with one another, were guided by an invisible hand that benefitted all calculating competitors. They were playing a positive-sum game.

Over time, economists creatively conceptualized analytical units at different levels of aggregation, stretching from individual economic man, to two interacting truckers and traders, to larger systems of such interactions, and then to aggregations (firms) followed by industries and eventually to the entire economy as envisioned, for example, by macroeconomic "accounting formulae" such as $Y = C + S + I$. Presumably, each level or unit of analysis could possibly have its own emerging properties.

Poovey began her analysis with how early moral philosophers attempted to create order out of the unknown. They proposed their own understanding of how markets worked. And, as already indicated, markets were seen to involve exchange relations that invited attempts to classify the "exchangers" as well as the systems qua systems in which the exchanges were executed. But there were neither words nor adequate evidence to meet this challenge. Hence, the use of metaphors and conjectures both about the exchangers (economic man) and the exchange system (involving an invisible hand).

As mentioned earlier, it was conjectured that there was an economic man and that all such creatures were essentially the same in their monetary motivations in pursuit of personal wealth. In addition to assumptions about rationally calculating economic man (whether a farmer, banker, or trader), there was an assumed end or goal that the system qua system pursued: the accumulation of collective and individual wealth. This did not mean that there were no systems other than market ones. There were parallel political, social, and religious systems, each with their own vocabularies, operating rules, and agents. Yes, Adam Smith and others referred to these multiple systems and how they in fact often influenced economic men and markets. But economists narrowed their focus, privileging markets and the economic side of truckers and traders as a system *sui generis* superior to the other systems with their own peculiar value assumptions and members.

The exchanges among rational market calculators required easily and widely understood yardsticks for comparison purposes, such as a range of weights and measures, including currency units that valued and facilitated exchanges. That is, acts that could be numbered and compared were essential for a well-functioning exchange system. But none of these essentials existed during Adam Smith's life. He had no way to test the conjectured stories he was telling.

As Poovey and others explained, the real world does not explain itself. Words (a vocabulary) are needed (socially constructed). Moving from metaphor to reality required accepted definitions of relevant facts that in turn could be enumerated. The numbers could then be mathematically manipulated to test hypothesized relations among the multiple facts that economists created to represent real exchanges and those who made them.

Of course, this developmental history was not peculiar to economics. The humanities, social sciences, and traditional hard sciences share analogous histories. Each of these disciplines has its own history of assumptions, values, facts, and numbers invented to make sense of a narrow slice of the real world.[14] That does not mean that disciplines are limited to one mental model and one vocabulary alone. Values do matter, and they can shape the story that experts tell. The stories could and did differ. For example, mention was made earlier to Bernard Mandeville's "The Fable of the Bees" and its argument on how private vices can produce public benefits, a scenario at odds with Scottish Enlightenment thinkers, such as Adam Smith, who seemed to shy away for the term "vice." And, as will be mentioned again later, the trajectory of economies and societies were driven not just by selfish pecuniary gain but also by sexual desires (that were transacted with personal gains and social costs).

Never-ending beneficial additions to national and personal wealth were value-based fictions and conjectures.

Free will is another fiction, though one well worth valuing. Yes, we do live and act in rule-enforced systems, and yes we might all be considered puppets, but systems allow puppets to differ in their ability to exercise their supposed free will and, thus, who benefits most and least from exchanges.

Although not singled out for separate attention, it seems reasonable to suggest that the distribution of Adam Smith's wealth among economic men can influence how the exchange system operates and whether national wealth is less than what could be theoretically possible.

The Missing Invisible

The world probably never experienced the ideal market in which Adam Smith's ideal economic men exchanged among themselves under conditions of pure natural freedom. Economists cannot even agree on what the invisible hand means. In his *Erasing the Invisible Hand, Essays on the Elusive and Misused Concepts in Economics,* Warren Samuels,[15] according to one review, found that Amazon listed:

> 33,888 books discussing the invisible hand (2009). The annual rate of mentions rose from *very low* (1816–1938), but the decade (1990–1999) recorded eight times the level of mentions between 1942 and 1974 and nearly 20 percent higher than for 1980–1989 (pp. 18–19). In consequence, the invisible hand is now widely believed to be significant, and it has spread to other disciplines.[16]

But what does the invisible hand mean? The answer evidently is that it means whatever Alice means it to mean. According to Samuel,

> [i]t is very difficult to construct a consistent story about the invisible hand. Consider... (1) the array of some four dozen identities given the invisible hand by different authors, (2) the a dozen or so functions, each with numerous variations, performable in principle by each identity, (3) the huge number of possibilities and the unknown number of possible combinations that involve contradictions or inconsistencies that make no sense, (4) tautologies, (5) the large number of specific identities and function that have conceptual and/or substantive problems, and so on.[17]

Adam Smith wrote that individual economic men were "led by an invisible hand," not "as if by an invisible hand."[18]

Providential or not, economists over the centuries claimed that the invisible hand is the "central principle of classical political economy," the "core of traditional economics," "the basic propositions of neo-classical economies," the "heart of economics," and its "foundational concept."[19] For the ideologues, it is the "basis for arguing the superiority of free markets over politically controlled processes."[20]

The invisible hand does miracles, for it helps explain why there is order in markets and societies, why coordination has been automated and why markets tend toward equilibrium, harmony, benevolence, and optimality. One need not ask "who" decides who gets what, for the invisible hand provides the answer. And it is up to the righteous to assure that no one interferes with the wonders of the invisible hand. Governments in particular should take a hands-off posture, except to free and facilitate that invisible mystery.

That is certainly a heavy burden for a socially constructed phrase to carry, especially since there is little consensus on what the invisible hand actually means and whether it exists in the real world. Is this theology or science? Is the invisible hand the economists' jewel bead in the lotus blossom of power, the *Oṃ maṇi padme hūṃ*?

To outsiders who never experienced the rigorous rite de passage that degree-holding economists must survive, rational economic men under the control of an invisible hand is an essential handle that economists use to rotate the discipline's prayer wheel.

Even a broken clock is accurate at least twice a day. But, of course, many economists are often accurate in their predictions. This suggests that the discipline is certainly more than smoke and mirrors.

In the Crossfire

It is not surprising then that this discipline has come under criticism. For example, the sociologists Orlando Patterson and Ethan Fosse charged economics as being a "pseudo-science, one with a string of massive failures."[21] Yes, many economists themselves recognize these complaints. For example, Yale's Robert Shiller, a recent president of the American Economics Association, gave his professional colleagues a mixed review. In his *What Good Are Economists*, Shiller observed:

> Since the global financial crisis and recession of 2007–2009, criticism of the economics profession has intensified. The failure of all but a few professional economists to forecast the episode—the after effects of which still linger—has led many to question whether the economics profession contributes anything significant to society. If they were unable to foresee something so important to people's wellbeing, what good are they?[22]

But Shiller also listed some of his professions' policy and program innovations, including "emissions trading, the earned-income tax credit, low trade tariffs, welfare-to-work programs, more effective monetary policy, auctions of spectrum licenses, transport-sector deregulation, deferred-acceptance algorithms, enlightened antitrust policy, an all-volunteer military, and clever use of default options to promote saving for retirement." Yes, clever, imaginative, and no doubt valuable contributions, but many, both within and outside the economics profession, expect more, including better mathematically based forecasts.

Shiller has also addressed these expectations, especially when they are based on questionable (misguided) assumptions about rational markets: "The housing market is another matter. It is far less rational than even the often irrational stock market."[23]

Other economists have raised questions about their members' heavy reliance on mathematics. As noted earlier, mathematics has become the language of economics just as it is the language of science more generally. But numbers and the ways they are manipulated can be questioned, as they should. For example, at the recent annual meeting of economists, New York University (NYU)'s Paul Romer took issue with one Nobel Prize–winning colleague for his "mathiness" approach to "new growth theory," one that can presumably help map the future.[24]

Ideology in the Open

A potential problem arises when economists stray off the disciplinary farm to promote their well-paid ideological interests. William Easterly, a competent and respected economist, exemplifies this crossover danger. In addition to his bona fides as a professional economist and consultant, he also promotes the slanted ideology of a Washington-based advocacy organization. Suffice to recognize that other economists also cross the line when they promote the ideologies of their own favored causes.

To some economists, the opposite of rationality is the tyranny of experts (those who promote what they consider rational reforms), the title that Easterly adopts in his well-worth reading 2013 book with a subtitle *Economists, Dictators, and the Forgotten Rights of the POOR*.[25] He implies a simple overarching dichotomy between (1) Adam Smith–type economists who place faith in the wisdom of individual rational economic men and (2) the international developmental experts such as Gunnar Myrdal who advocate top-down rather than bottom-up approaches to how best to launch economic growth in poorer countries.

Development economists, according to Easterly, are more concerned with the welfare of the state than with the welfare of individuals. This leads to a "fondness for authority" and the ready use of coercion. Easterly emphasizes the dangers of an intrusive state but largely ignores fundamental questions about the purpose and nature of the state.

Conscious design, according to Easterly, is inferior to spontaneous solutions by individual actors free from state coercion. Development agencies, he argues, should restrain the power of the state in order to allow wise rational economic men to make their own decisions. The best social engineering would avoid manipulation. Moreover, big brother, whether in a multi- or single-state development form, can stifle rather than encourage economic growth.

Spontaneous order and spontaneous solutions are superior to conscious design. That is the wonder of rational economic men and the rational markets these rational men would create if the state would just get out of the way.

Defoe's pre–Adam Smith negative depiction of economic man was a relic of the past even within the poorest of the poor countries that Easterly observed during his overseas development assignments.

Easterly has great faith in selfish economic man trucking and trading under the watchful invisible hand of socially sanctioned oversight intended to assure level playing fields and honesty. He, Easterly, favors "systems that nobody designed, that display order that nobody ordered [the invisible hand], and that deliver outcomes that nobody intended." In partial support of his assumptions, he favorably quotes Kenneth Arrow's statement that "the notion that through the workings of an entire system effects may be very different from, and even opposed to, intentions is surely the most important contribution that economic thought has made to the general understanding of social processes."[26] And as Lawrence Summers approvingly wrote: "the invisible hand is more powerful than the [un]hidden hand. Things will happen in well-organized efforts without direction, controls, plans. That's the Hayek legacy."

Unflinching the invisible hand assumes that there will be no war of all against all and that life will not be nasty, brutish, and short.

According to some critics, that is all balderdash.

Easterly's school of economic thought seems to assume that a shadow of providential design still operates today and that all will be rewarded if public authorities just retire from the scene. In sha'Allah!

The best state, it seems, is no state—at least in so far as how trucking and trading goes. And the rights of individuals always trump the rights of the state, whatever the state means independently of the citizens within it. The state is depicted as a foreign Leviathan that is no longer justified.

It does not represent citizens; it represents those who hold state power, whether visible or not. (Yes, there is much mainline support for this claim. James Ferguson's *The Anti-Politics Machine* is an excellent read, one that, again, explores how international economic development experts socially constructed a false value-based reality.[27])

In further support of his argument, Easterly references Dani Rodrik's 2007 survey of policies and growth in which he concluded that "the experience of the last two decades has frustrated the expectations...[that] we had a good fix on the policies that promote growth."

While Easterly's *The Tyranny of Experts* includes many well-worth insights, his view of markets misrepresents what development programs and experts actually do. At least that has been my four years' experience working on social development challenges in Hong Kong and South East Asia in the 1960s, followed by nearly two decades dealing with a broad range of economic and social development challenges during the 1980s and later in Egypt, Yemen, and Guinea-Bissau. Yes, all three of these Arab and African states were failures in many respects despite the well-designed international development programs supporting changes that are friendly to individual initiative and improvements in the welfare of communities and their members.

If not dangerous, it is mischievous and misleading to pigeon-hole reform initiatives as either good (working to expand freedom of choice) or bad (strengthening the power of the state).[28] This is a false dichotomy. Moreover, the invisible hand is limited to the trucking and trading of private goods, not to public goods such as roads, education, and all the other components of social, legal, and physical infrastructure supporting and facilitating private exchanges. The promising future of the "free man" that economists from Adam Smith to William Easterly have conjectured will likely depend on how well the external state is able to structure and control markets in which Defoe's selfish, avarice-driven economic men truck and trade with one another:

> No man is an island,
> Entire of itself,
> Every man is a piece of the continent,
> A part of the main.
> If a clod be washed away by the sea,
> Europe is the less.
> As well as if a promontory were.

As well as if a manor of thy friend's
Or of thine own were:
Any man's death diminishes me,
Because I am involved in mankind,
And therefore never send to know for whom the bell tolls;
It tolls for thee.

John Donne

Adam Smith certainly agreed with John Donne. Yes, there was the avarice-driven rational economic man, but he could thrive only by fairly trucking and trading with other similarly selfish economic men. Taking unfair advantage of an exchange would distort the distribution of benefits, and with political influence, this distortion could metastasize into an unbalanced distribution exchange system that favored some to the disadvantage of others. In doing so, markets could fall short of realizing the potential wealth of the nation. Distribution of wealth (inequality) can matter.

Both modern and historical economic dictionaries and theories are infused with value assumptions. One purpose of the present exercise has been to identify and document some of these questionable assumptions. I do not, however, provide alternative mental models and vocabularies. That challenge is well beyond the limited capabilities of a near-deaf 86-year-old noneconomist.

Perhaps, the market that Adam Smith envisioned could avoid the perpetual (yes, perpetual) manias, bubbles, business cycles, underused human and material resources, high rates of pain and unemployment, bankruptcies, and all the other challenges that economies have suffered over the centuries. Certainly, Smith's ideal is attractive if in fact the closer that an economy is to Adam Smith's mental model the better everyone will be. No bubbles and cycles in such an ideal world, and everyone would be monetarily rewarded according to the monetary value of what they contribute through trucking-and-trading.

Although we can only guess (conjecture) about an ideal, never-calibrated market, thanks to Poovey, we have a better understanding of the attempts to ground mental models in facts and numbers that would best reflect the real world (and how it might change if constraints on it were removed). Again, the history of economics, argues Poovey, includes the history of categories, facts that capture the essential feature(s) of categories, and the way that facts become numbers that allow the testing of hypotheses, the creation of assumed economic laws, and the construction of multivariable computer models. But, as we will see in the following chapter, value judgments were made in constructing measures of wealth (in this case, Gross National Product and related concepts). Economists do not seem able to avoid moral sentiments.

Notes

1. Among the great many relevant books and articles on Smith in addition to what Poovey has written are David Warsh, *Knowledge and the Wealth of Nations: A Story of Economic Discovery* (Norton, 2007) and his blog *Economics Principals* at http://www.economicprincipals.com/. Also R. F. Brissenden (1969) "Authority, Guilt, and Anxiety in *The Theory of Moral Sentiments.*" *Texas Studies in Literature and Language*, 11, 2, pp 945–962; N. Chomsky, (2002). *Understanding Power: The Indispensible Chomsky*. The New Press (p.221ff). A. Fitzgibbons, (1995), *Adam Smith's System of Liberty, Wealth and Virtue*. Oxford: Clarendon Press. E. Rothschild, (2001), *Economic sentiments: Adam Smith, Condorcet, and the Enlightenment*. Cambridge: Harvard University Press. E. Rothschild, E. and A. Sen, (2006) "Adam Smith's Economics" in K. Haakonssen, (ed.) *The Cambridge Companion to Adam Smith*. Cambridge: Cambridge University Press, pp 319–65. A. Sen, (2010) "Introduction." In Smith, A. (2010) [1759] *The Theory of Moral Sentiments* (Hanley, R.P. [ed.]). London: Penguin, pp 9–27.
2. Many social scientists have criticized concepts of human nature. E.g., Marshall Sahlins concluded that Western society has been built on a perverse and mistaken idea of human nature. Among his multiple relevant contributions, see his *The Western Illusion of Human Nature: With Reflections on the Long History of Hierarchy, Equality and the Sublimation of Anarchy in the West, and...Conceptions of the Human Condition* (Prickly Paradigm Press, 2008).
3. He presumably found this example in the French *Encyclopédie*, tom. v. (published in 1755), *s.v.*Épingle as ascribed to M. Delaire, "qui décrivait la fabrication de l'épingle dans les ateliers même des ouvriers," p. 807. In some factories, the division was carried further to 25 separate operations. E. Chambers, *Cyclopædia*, vol. ii., 2nd ed., 1738, and 4th ed., 1741, *s.v.* See http://www.econlib.org/library/Smith/smWN1.html.
4. Joseph Stiglitz, "Celebrating the Irrational" *Project Syndicate* (December 11, 2002).
5. Hans Zetterberg (op. cit), among others, argued that "[e]conomy, with its focus on wealth, uses mostly evaluative language; it is not the goods

and services we have that constitute our riches, but their evaluation." See his Table 2.1 Abbreviated Preview of a Periodic Table of Societal Realms (comparing how different disciplines label and understand such concepts as rewards, freedom, rationality, and mobilization, among many others). He also states that "[o]ur Propositions about social reality are not the same as Laws of nature. The latter are immutable, and calculations and forecasts based on these command credibility; they are genuine predictions. By contrast, certainty is absent in our Propositions about social reality; they are all probabilistic, and they can even be negated or altered by social designs employed by rulers and by free people—but only at a cost and with a human effort."

6. Stiglitz, 61.
7. *The Edinburgh Review* created in 1802 is sometimes referenced as the first publication with serious analyses of the economy. It wasn't until 1891 that the first England-based academic source on economics (*The Economic Journal*) appeared, five years after the American economists initiated *The Quarterly Journal of Economics* in 1886, four years before Marshall's 1890 *Principles*. See my *Concise History* for more background on the early literature and assumptions of the founders of modern economics.
8. Karl Popper also emphasized the need for theories to be stated in ways that can withstand a test for their falsifiability.
9. Florian Schui, *Austerity: The Great Failure* (Yale, 2015).
10. "Incrementalism won't cure these crises," *Washington Post Op-Ed* (July 12, 2015).
11. The butterfly effect, according to chaos theory, is the sensitive dependence on initial conditions in which a small change in one state of a deterministic nonlinear system can result in large differences in a later state. See James Gleick, *Chaos: Making a New Science* (Penguin, 2008).
12. Richard E. Neustadt and Ernest R. May, *Thinking in Time: The Uses of History for Decision Makers* (Free Press, 1986), 152–53.
13. The original first full title was *The Life and Strange Surprizing Adventures of Robinson Crusoe, of York, Mariner: Who Lived Eight and Twenty Years, All Alone in an Un-inhabited Island on the Coast of America, near the Mouth of the Great River of Oroonoque; Having Been Cast on Shore by Shipwreck, Wherein All the Men Perished But Himself. With an Account How He Was At Last As Strangely Deliver'd by Pyrates.*
14. For an interesting historical account of how social scientists have attempted to distinguish social from cultural systems, see William H. Sewall Jr. *Logics of History: Social Theory and Social Transformation* (Chicago Studies in Practices of Meaning) 2005.
15. Warren Samuels, *Erasing the Invisible Hand, Essays on the Elusive and Misused Concepts in Economics* (Cambridge, 2011).

16. EH. Net February 2012.
17. Samuels, xvii.
18. Ibid., 7.
19. Ibid., 10.
20. Ibid., 12.
21. Orlando Patterson and Ethan Fosse, "Overreliance on the Pseudo-Science of Economics, "*New York Times Opinion Pages*, February 9, 2015. Other contributors to this debate organized by the *Times* titled their pieces "Exceptions Overwhelm Economic Rules, 'Analyze and Explain, Don't Prognosticate'," "The Failures of Economics Shouldn't Obscure Widespread Success," and "Economists' Ambivalent Authority," all available online at http://www.nytimes.com/roomfordebate/2015/02/09/are-economists-overrated.
22. Robert Shiller, "What Good Are Economists" (*Project Syndicate*, January 15, 2015).
23. Robert Shiller, "The Housing Market Still Isn't Rational," *New York Times*, July 26, 2015.
24. *See his blog "Mathiness and Academic Identity," May 27, 2015 at http://paulromer.net/mathiness-and-academic-identity/ and http://paulromer.net/mathiness/ Another site quotes Romer as follows: "[M]athiness is a critique of a style that lets economists draw invalid inferences from the assumptions and structure of a model; a style that authors can use to persuade the reader (and themselves) to adopt conclusions that do not follow by the rules of logic; a style that tolerates wishful thinking instead of precise, clearly articulated reasoning. The mathiness that I point to in the Lucas (2009) paper and in the follow up paper by Lucas and Moll (2014) involves hand-waving and verbal evasion that is the exact opposite of the precision in reasoning and communication exemplified by Debreu/Bourbaki, and I'm for precision and clarity." http://www.bruegel.org/nc/blog/detail/article/1641-mathiness-in-economics/ Along the same lines, Rodrik references Kenneth Boulding's observation: "Mathematics brought rigor to economics; unfortunately it also brought mortis" (Rodrik, op. cit., 11). His book has many other useful insights supportive of the present analysis (that was authored well before Rodrik published his own contribution). See, e.g., his discussion of economic theories as fables and parables—and his reference to Galbraith's economics statement that God created economic forecasters to make astrologers look good.*
25. William Easterly, The Tyranny of Experts (Basic Books, 2015).
26. Also known as the law of unanticipated consequences—or serendipity, an historical concept that Robert K. Merton and Elinor Barber explored in their *The Travels and Adventures of Serendipity: A Study in Sociological Semantics and the Sociology of Science* (Princeton, 2006).
27. James Ferguson, *The Anti-Politics Machine* (University of Minnesota Press, 1994).

28. In the late 1970s, I was a codesigner in Egypt of the very successful Neighborhood Urban Services Project, a large key component of a $600 million decentralization program designed to support administrative decentralization, increase public participation in local government, strengthen local government capability to deliver services, and improve the quality of life for urban residents. I was not responsible for managing the project, but in another office within the United States Agency for International Development (USAID) mission, I designed and implemented projects delivering technical and productivity services to small and larger industrial firms, primarily private but also public (except for those in the military sector). My responsibilities in Yemen were for initiatives to strengthen local capabilities to deliver health, water, and child survival services; for initiatives to strengthen independent business groups and free markets; for a first-ever major women-in-development economic program; and for support for independent legislative and judicial institutions, the same thrusts I pursued in Guinea-Bissau in the early 1990s before that country became a narco-state. For a review of some of my work in Hong Kong, see my "Donald Tsang's Proposed Family Policy Commission: Lessons from Hong Kong and American Experiences," *The Hong Kong Journal of Social Work*, 41: 1 & 2 (Summer and Winter 2007). This article benefitted from my numerous books and articles based on four years of research in the then colony of Hong Kong as well as my role in initiating and directing the joint Governor [Askew] and Legislative Florida Task Force on Marriage and the Family Unit as well as the multiyear Governor's Task Force on Housing and Community Development. The family initiative was among the first American efforts to explore the possibility of a national family policy. On behalf of the National Council on Family Relations, I headed a national task force on family policies related to President Nixon's proposed Family Assistance Plan that included a guaranteed minimum family income. On behalf of the Council, I testified before Congress on this proposed but never-accepted legislation.

CHAPTER 5

Value Judgments Regarding the Meaning of Wealth

Abstract Adam Smith's title phrase "wealth of the nation" pointed to the end point of the economist's map to nirvana. But what is wealth, how do you measure it, and should the distribution of wealth be considered along with the sum total of whatever wealth means?

Measures of national income and product (wealth) are moral statistics. Questions are raised not just about what to measure but also how wealth is distributed among those who create it. Competing moral measurements are discussed along with what is meant by the economy, why some features (categories) are important measures of the stock of wealth and the key drivers behind changes in this stock. These conceptual and measurement challenges require value as well as analytical decisions.

Keywords National account • National product • National wealth • Welfare • Ideology • Measure • Moral decisions • Winners • Losers • Moral statistics • Distribution • Progress • Stock

There are alternative ways to measure the morally-tinged concepts of wealth, income, and growth. We now have competing value-based measurements.

Everyone presumably wants to add to the nation's wealth. To know whether forward progress is being made toward that goal, it is necessary

© The Editor(s) (if applicable) and the Author(s) 2016

R.E. Mitchell, *The Language of Economics*,
DOI 10.1007/978-3-319-33981-8_5

to define what wealth means and its key components so that facts and measures (numbers) can be assembled.

Other decisions are also necessary. For example, economists are challenged to clarify what they mean by the economy, why some features (categories) are important measures of the stock of wealth and the key drivers behind changes in this stock as well.

Addressing these conceptual and measurement challenges requires value as well as analytical decisions, all guided by the assumed purposes or rationale for focusing on economies and changes in them.

An argument can be made that just as economies change (and that they have), so must the categories used to dissect and understand them. Adam Smith's world had already changed by the time Alfred Marshall authored his *Principles of Economics.* Marshall's world quickly evolved by the time John Maynard Keynes wrote on the macro economy.

This chapter explores some of the not-so-hidden value assumptions made in selecting measures for the socially constructed concept of national wealth (income and product). Economics, again, is not value-neutral.

What to Measure

America's first generally accepted measure of national wealth (Gross National Product [GNP] and its variations) was Simon Kuznets' 1934 contribution based on a mass production economy quite different from what we have today. Yes, economists and others invented new terms and measures, but these still require that value decisions be made.

So just as historians are said to invent history, economists invent the economy.

Adam Smith considered the service sector to be unproductive, so many of those who are reading this paragraph are, in Adam Smith's mind, drags rather than drivers of markets. The Russian communists shared the same assumption. Services, however, are estimated to account for up to two-thirds or more of our contemporary American economy. If Keynes and others are correct in claiming that financial sector's casino-game capitalists (a not-insignificant portion of the overall financial "service" sector) detract rather than add to the wealth of the nation, then official measures of their activities would be assigned negative rather than positive values!

That is not what measures of wealth in the form of GNP and income do.[1] They are locked into value decisions carried over from earlier times when economies were different, as were, perhaps, national policy challenges over time.

Our first national accounts were for a mass production economy, not for today's world with rapid innovations and intangible (e.g., digital) services.[2] Measures of physical and service "stock" rather than flows raise conceptual questions not so visible in older economies.

I have drawn on two useful historical reviews of how values and measures changed over time. First are the articles included in the Russell Sage Foundation edited volume by William Alonso and Paul Starr: *The Politics of Numbers*.[3] Second is Diane Coyle's *GDP, A Brief Affectionate History*,[4] also an invaluable history.

Starr, noted:

> At issue in the design of national accounts are fundamental questions of policy, not just of fact. In the early debate over the accounts, Simon Kuznets repeatedly emphasized the practical impossibility of measuring national product without making philosophical choices about the end-purpose of economic activity...estimators had no choice but to make explicit philosophical choices. (43)

Whether consciously made or not, the choices required political judgments about the role of markets in the health of the larger state. This led to decisions about appropriate categories, facts representing these categories, and measures that are sensitive to changes in the larger economy. Subsequent analyses could weed out indicators and measures that were poor predictors of changes in the larger economy, however that concept was operationalized.

"Truth chains" were being invented and reinvented. These chains and the values underlying them help shape how economists and others view and understand markets:

> Official statistics do not merely hold a mirror to reality. They reflect presuppositions and theories about the nature of reality. They are products of social, political, and economic interests that are often in conflict with each other. And they are sensitive to methodological decisions made by complex organizations with limited resources. Moreover, official numbers, especially those that appear in series, often do not reflect all these factors instantaneously: They echo their past as the surface of a landscape reflects its underlying geology.[5]

National economic accounts and figures are social constructs, the lens that reveals the world that those who promoted the accounts wish us to see and accept.

Instead of (moral) statistics on health, education, individual well-being, and the distribution of national wealth, we are to focus on aggregate economic numbers and the components that are assumed to account for them. By choice, certain economic activities are not measured. For example, services provided by homemakers within the family are ignored. They and other nonmarket services are not worthy components of the national economy.

National economic and other policies take notice of official aggregate statistics, for they somehow indicate the status and trends in national welfare as politically defined.

Again, Simon Kuznets, among others, realized that value judgments were being made: any "view of national income as a *net* product total… can be defined only in relation to *some end-goal of economic activity.*"[6] That does not mean, however, that other statistical information does not exist on various assumed components of well-being, such as vital statistics, employment and unemployment, inflation, student performance, hunger, crime, consumer confidence, and, yes, happiness and satisfaction—all among the statistics provided by a vast public and private sector information industry. These numbers and the ways they are interpreted comprise the political arithmetic of our day.

That array, according to Kuznets, could include measures of national "economic *welfare*," not just output. But, as it turned out, today's Gross Domestic Product (GDP) numbers are not measures of welfare nor of well-being. The meanings assigned to national economic growth may implicitly address welfare, but welfare raises a host of value-related measurement challenges not yet adequately understood nor addressed, at least according to some critics. (See Coyle for her coverage of these challenges.)

Whatever these numbers measure, the term "national income" is not what Coyle labeled a "primary fact" but instead are an "empirical construct." Different definitions and measurements would be necessary to capture the status of national welfare and well-being.

Still, the empirical construct we now have is, according to many economists, a useful tool for understanding and managing the national economy.

Alternatives

If one prefers alternative measures based on other value assumptions, they can be found as well. For example, some internationally attuned development experts suggest a "dashboard approach" such as Australia's annual *Measuring Australia's Progress* or the Organisation for Economic Co-operation and Development (OECD)'s *Better Life Index* (available online).[7] Others have argued that "the real measure of the performance of an economy is how well the typical family does." In America, there has been zero growth in this measure over the past quarter century.[8] Angus Deaton is well worth reading for his challenging alternative measures.[9] He is centrally concerned with "the measurement of wellbeing…the heart" of his *The Great Escape*. "Life evaluation scores" rather than income or other dashboard measures are introduced to tap how people see their own lives. Neither income nor GDP individually or aggregated adequately captures the meaning of well-being. His measures, he recognizes, introduce value judgments of "social standards of decency."

Yes, according to Stiglitz, "a rising tide lifted all yachts," but inequality is at a rate not seen in three-quarters of a century. (More questions about the value-laden term "inequality" will be explored later.)

Decisions have been made on what to count, why to count, and the meaning of the counted "facts," even though critics have charged that these facts provide "specious accuracy."[10]

Economists have had to make many value judgments—for example, whether and how to measure public goods and military expenditures in a privately dominated market. Should government expenditures be considered investments or consumptions? And what about negative externalities such as pollution or traffic congestion?

There are many essential contributions that governments make in today's private-oriented markets. Moral, political, and economic decisions have to be made on what, why, and how to count these contributions. Changes in definitions and counting procedures can provide alternative scenarios of contemporary economies and trends within them. Some critics would no doubt welcome metrics that combine economic and other themes along the lines of the title to Edward Banfield's *The Moral Basis of a Backward Society* (1958). Yes, "moral statistics," perhaps an oxymoron, but certainly not the first paradox within the make-believe world of economists.

Mark Twain is credited with popularizing the observation that there are "lies, damned lies, and statistics," a phrase describing the persuasive power of numbers, particularly the use of statistics that are used to bolster weak arguments. It is also sometimes colloquially used to doubt statistics used to prove an opponent's point. Perhaps, Twain was far back in Keynes' mind when he wrote: "When the facts change, I change my mind. What do you do, sir?"[11] This question and the answers to it arise in the course of measuring national wealth and income, a game of politics that includes the politics of evidence and values.

The Social Creation of Systems

Economists had to create classification systems, "the ordering or arrangement of objects into groups or sets on the basis of their relationships." Classification "really involves or is a part of the formation of hypotheses as to the nature of things." This entire process requires inventing and defining domains, groupings, labels ("to count 'homelessness' rather than 'vagrancy' is the statistical counterpart to transforming deviants into victims"), followed by ordering and quantified displays. (See the earlier references to Mary Poovey's two books.)

Measurement and weighting are additional value-laden challenges, not just technical ones, for facts just do not speak for themselves. They are socially created with implied purposes that give priority to what Adam Smith labeled the wealth of a nation, not the well-being of all who contribute to and consume that wealth—or are harmed by certain wealth-creating activities such as negative externalities.

Some forms of wealth and the processes of producing them are not easily placed within an economy based on individuals who truck and trade with one another. Private wealth and public goods, as well as positive and negative externalities, should, in theory at least, be incorporated in assessing the wealth of a nation as well as how that wealth is distributed throughout society.

Measuring goods is an easier challenge than measuring ideas, knowledge, and services. The unmeasurable can become the hypothesized unknown, such as will be noted later with regard to what Robert Solow and others labeled "technical progress" and its contribution to increases in the nation's wealth.

Again, those who measure national wealth have had to make a good number of decisions on what and why to include or exclude categories, facts, and numbers from what is being measured. Some critics of the focus and components of national wealth argue that ideas are what really matters in contemporary knowledge-based economies. And ideas are not necessarily tradables nor traceables. They defy measurement.

National accounts that include measures of income and product are the modern carryover of the political arithmetic associated with Sir William Petty's (1623–1687) surveys of his vast Irish landholdings. (See Mary Poovey for an excellent history of what drove Petty to conduct these number-based studies and why the monarchy did not adopt his innovative political arithmetic.)

Watch Your Values

If economists fail to appreciate the value implications of their numbers, politicians are not similarly blind. For example, when numbers posed a threat to his voodoo economic theories, President Ronald Reagan (it is alleged) disbanded the Office of Federal Statistical Policy and Standards "and moved toward cutting the funds available for statistical programs more generally."[12] He wasn't the only world leader to disapprove of statistics. In the early 1970s, Russia stopped publishing data on infant mortality. Some climate change deniers today follow the Russian example.

Professionals who fail to recognize that their facts are not welcomed by elected leaders imprisoned in value containers can also suffer:

> The peculiar problem of official forecasts is that they serve not only to predict future states but also to proclaim present intentions. An administration that intends to "stay the course" is not likely to tolerate forecasts by its own chief economist indicating that current policy will lead to slow growth and high deficits. So it was that Martin Feldstein had to leave his post as chairman of the Council of Economic Advisors in the Reagan administration—and so it was that President Reagan nearly abolished the council. (Alonso and Starr, 49)

President Reagan was neither the first nor the last to live in a bubble of imaginary markets based on imagined values, not the real world, as their critics have argued. In his *Peddling Prosperity*, Paul Krugman touches on the value-blinders worn by proponents of different economic policies that are still alive today in Washington advocacy centers. Number-crunching economists can still be blind to the changing world around them. Old catechisms still haunt the discipline.

Gaps Discovered

Yes, normal economic theories, concepts, and implied moral values have evolved over time. And measurement problems have been and continue to be recognized along with the questionable assumptions economists make.[13] For example, Robert Solow and others (as noted earlier) discovered in 1940 that "the great majority of postwar GDP growth was 'explained' by 'technical progress', that is, by the "one part of the theory that had no economic explanation." [14] Economic models based on a mass production system could not capture the central features and processes found in our knowledge-based present.

Knowledge and related concepts of technology were exogenous to traditional growth models and the mental as well as value assumptions they implied. By 1957, according to Solow and others, four-fifths of the growth of US output per worker was attributable to technical progress, a residual category as visible at the invisible hand. It is as though economists were returning to Mandeville's beehive with a new genus of technologists working along with workers and drones to add to the queen's and the hive's survival-with-growth. Certainly, trucking and trading of marketable goods was no longer a sufficient model for understanding markets and changes in them.

Economists know this, and much attention has been given to operationalizing knowledge and those who either produce or use it.[15] But the discipline of economics still seems focused on Adam Smith's end objective: adding to the wealth of a nation.

We turn next to alternative value assumptions about what economies are supposed to accomplish.

Notes

1. GDP (Gross Domestic Product) and GNP (Gross National Product) differ, with the first referring to all "final" goods and services produced in a country in a single year, and the latter to the "market value" of all goods and services produced in the year by labor and property supplied by the residents of a country. Gross National Income (GNI) has other components. Since these national totals are the dependent variables that economists explore and explain (predict), it seems prudent to distinguish among these different national indicators of the movement and status of the national economy. The same definitional qualifications apply to other ingredients in the discussions and formulae that economists use. The vari-

ety and differences among short-hand titles that are attached to national totals contribute to the confusion and mischief of competing analyses and conclusions that one reads in the public and professional economic press. (Or am I the only one to be confused and on guard?)

2. One of my first mass production jobs was with the fast-moving conveyer-driven axels passing by me in the Chevy Gear & Axel factory located in Hamtramck, Michigan (really part of Detroit). Poet Lauriat Philip Levine worked in the same factory several years after me (and presumably after our union, the United Automobile Workers [UAW], insisted on safety and other improvements). He described this factory out of the past as a "hell-hole." See his "Nobody's Detroit" in *Detroit Disassembled* (Damiani/Akron Art Museum, 2010) by Andrew Moore and Philip Levine. While I shared the frightening features of this factory, I was also fascinated by how the long converging assembly lines rooted individual drones in place to manipulate rapidly passing metal parts that today can be attached by robots. Chevy Gear & Axle was a parts plant, not one for final assembly that requires more physical movement and mental agility by workers. (I worked in these factories as well.) We drones were directed by moving metal conveyor belts outside our control to perform repetitive, physically demanding, and often dangerous tasks. I was a tool that conveyor belts manipulated. Working on my uncle's mid-state farm (a family farm started by my maternal grandparents in the 1800s) was an entirely different type of experience, one that depended on individual decisions and initiatives. Yes, the Talmud and other religious texts may chant that great is work for it honors the workman, but trading one's efforts in return for a living can have very different meanings.
3. Russell Sage Foundation, 1984.
4. Princeton, 2014. Also well worth reading is "The trouble with GDP" in the April 30, 2016 issue of *The Economist.*
5. Alonso and Starr, 1.
6. Ibid., 147.
7. "There is more to life than the cold numbers of GDP and economic statistics—This Index allows you to compare well-being across countries, based on 11 topics the OECD has identified as essential, in the areas of material living conditions and quality of life." http://www.oecdbetterlifeindex.org/#/11111111111.
8. Stiglitz, op. cit., 13–14.
9. Op. cit., xuv, 7–8, 17, 46, 51, 170.
10. Alonso and Starr op. cit., 190. While an undergraduate at the University of Michigan in the late 1940s and early 1950s, the author was a coder and editor for the university's Survey Research Center, the host for George Katona's consumer expectations national surveys, an initiative that later became the

national Consumer Sentiment Index included in the Leading Indicator Composite Index published by the US Department of Commerce's Bureau of Economic Analysis. (The author later directed two of the additional four survey research centers he joined—five in total.) The objectives of the Composite Index are to assess near-time consumer attitudes on the business climate, personal finance, and spending; to promote an understanding of, and to forecast changes in, the national economy; to provide a means of incorporating empirical measures of consumer expectations into models of spending and saving behavior; to gauge the economic expectations and probable future spending behavior of the consumer; and to judge the consumer's level of optimism/pessimism. The present author has been exploring measurement challenges over the years. For example, see his "Survey Materials Collected in the Developing Countries: Sampling, Measurement, and Interviewing Obstacles to Intra-and Inter-National Comparisons," in *International Social Science Journal*, 17:4, 1965 and reprinted variously, including in Donald Warwick and Samuel Osherson, eds., *Comparative Research Methods* (Prentice-Hall, 1973).

11. There are different sources for this quotation, one that may have been: "When my information changes, I alter my conclusions. What do you do, sir?" The quote in the text is included in Jennifer Homans' edited *When the Facts Change: Essays, 1995–2010, Tony Judt* (Penguin, 2015).
12. Alonso and Starr, 185–86.
13. See Jonathan Schlefer, op. cit., along with my own *The Assumptions Economists Make About Markets.*
14. [Coyle, 56] David Warsh, *Knowledge and the Wealth of Nations: A Story of Economic Discovery* provides a good coverage of these relatively recent developments in what economists think. Warsh's blog *Economics Principles* http://www.economicprincipals.com/ is a worthy source on the history of recent economic theories and the economists who make them. The American Economics Association has a list of economists' blogs at http://rfe.org/showCat.php?cat_id=96.
15. Barry Bosworth, according to a Brookings Institution blog, "has shown that a lot of productivity gains are occurring in the service sector and that it isn't just capital deepening that is producing these gains. It is everything from better management to human capital investment and organizational innovation—all the things we cannot measure very well but which show up in the data as an unexplained residual." Isabel Sawhill, "Whatever happened to middle class income gains?" July 7, 2015, Brookings Blog. http://www.brookings.edu/research/opinions/2015/07/01-middle-class-income-gains-sawhill.

CHAPTER 6

Alternative Values and Mental Models: The Recurring Challenge of Inequality

Abstract Compound interest calculations raise questions about the focus that economists place on measures of wealth, product, and income. Many parts of our current cultural, economic, and political rainbow are being reexamined. Thomas Malthus and others believed there was a limit to the growth of national and personal wealth. Ever-increasing happiness and welfare was a hoax perpetuated by economists.

Economists, of course, have not been blind to the absence of wealth—that is, to poverty. But the way economists ask questions about poverty calls for responses using the moral language of the discipline. Ask an economics question and you get an economics answer. Underlying value biases are ignored as being outside the expertise of the discipline.

Keywords Happiness and misery • Limit to growth • Hoax • Moral language • Bias • Inequality • Thomas Malthus • Poverty

It has taken time for economists to change the ways they ask questions about poverty and increasingly about inequality. But some members of the discipline now seem to be on the road to rethinking the moral basis of their field of expertise.

© The Editor(s) (if applicable) and the Author(s) 2016

R.E. Mitchell, *The Language of Economics*,
DOI 10.1007/978-3-319-33981-8_6

Myths Are Rediscovered

Enlightenment thinkers were optimistic about a future in which rational self-aware citizens were freed of their feudal and religious shackles. The new end of the rainbow was personal and national wealth, neither of which depended on providential design. Personal virtue was important but not measurable. Only personal wealth was the measure of all things, including one's own social standing.

Of course, there were always critics who questioned the values and arithmetic of the new breed of economists. Many preferred older value-based ethics over new real-life numbers and facts. Different descriptions became different prescriptions and proscriptions. But according to some historians, it seems that Enlightenment values and the new science of the subjective mind along with assumptions about universal human nature helped remove the shackles of the past, thereby paving the way for a new civic and market arithmetic.

At the time, simple arithmetic might have helped—for example, compound interest calculations should have been enough to raise questions about the assumptions made by some economists, as recently suggested by Cesar Hidalgo:

> As do many others, I believe that the idea of economic growth is ready for retirement. The lingering question is what will replace it, since economic growth will leave a void in public speech, as both a staple paragraph of political campaigns and a recurrent topic in news media. But economic growth cannot last forever. If the GDP per capita in the United States grew in real terms at a modest rate of 1 percent for the next millennium, the average American would be making a whopping $1.1 billion annually by the year 3014. A more reasonable interpretation of this number is to think of the growth during the last century as part of an S-shaped curve, a phase transition. This means either that growth will peter out during this millennium or that we're measuring the wrong thing. Either way, we can conclude that the idea of economic growth is on its way out.[1]

What then might replace growth?

The Malthus Alternative

Have economists been chasing the wrong target since Adam Smith? What or what else should economists and others be measuring and conceptualizing? Is there any way to escape the value-burdened mental shades we all wear? And are there mental models and values that compete with those invented by Adam Smith?[2]

Yes, there were and are alternatives to Smith. One of these was offered by Thomas Malthus (1766–1834), author of *Essay on the Principle of Population*, first published in 1798 followed by many revised and vastly expanded editions.

Writing from the perspective of theological utilitarianism, Malthus accumulated scattered population numbers (he had to travel to Scandinavia for these, although his later editions drew on an increasing supply of English sources) that he added to apparently hypothetical numbers on food supplies to feed the population. That is, he had a two-variable model: the number of mouths to feed (population) and the amount of food to fill those mouths. The former increased at a geometric rate because men were not only trucking and trading goods but were also deeply engaged in the commerce of sex with their wives.

Population numbers were a variable; food supplies were less so. They only increased at an arithmetical rate well behind the geometrical growth rate of mouths to feed. This meant that Adam Smith's material wealth could not, through "God's providential design," carry all members of society and society itself on an ever-upward climb toward material accumulation and heavenly bliss. Rational economic men trucking and trading could not, for technical reasons, significantly increase the supply of edibles. And the assumed salvation of international trade was a nonstarter, according to Malthus.

Adam Smith was wrong to confuse wealth with happiness and the welfare of all. He was also wrong to narrowly focus on the hypothetical calculating rational economic man who pursued material holdings to the exclusion of other pursuits, including those that took place in the bedroom. He thereby was blind to the "perpetual oscillation between happiness and misery," according to Malthus.

But what Malthus actually saw around him (as explained by Poovey) "were not signs of progressive improvement but human suffering and pain." And "God inflicted the principle of population upon them; in order to wrest spirit out of the fallen flesh, he made suffering the daily lot of humankind."[3] This was certainly what Frenchmen experienced during their revolution of the 1790s, "a perpetual oscillation between happiness and misery."

A balancing bar operated in England as well. This was part of God's population plan that he inflicted on man in order to "wrest spirit out of the fallen flesh, he made suffering the daily lot of humankind."[4] Or as

Deaton observed, "death and deprivation kept the population in check, but even for the survivors, the conditions of life were terrible," as measured by weight, height, and life expectancy estimates. "The Malthusian imperative trades off more people for shorter people."[5]

Adam Smith evidently did not share the same values placed within a mental model that assumed that poverty and pain were inherent in the general laws created by Malthus' Supreme Being. Smith saw inevitable progress toward materially based happiness, a win-win race for all and for society at large. Malthus, on the other hand, thought there were limits on possible progress. These limits would destructively fall especially hard on the general population, not on those at the top of society, who had the material wherewithal to outbid the masses in markets for food to feed their gluttonous mouths.

Economists since Adam Smith and before were certainly aware of widespread poverty. It had been a public issue since at least 1622 following "flagrant protests against conditions that had been making the poor poorer since Elizabeth's reign."[6]

Poovey (p. 295) places the Smith–Malthus difference in the context of what historians consider the Malthus–Ricardo debate over two questions:

> Was national well-being primarily a matter of "wealth" or of "happiness"? And by what method should political economists generate knowledge?

Malthus, as quoted by Poovey, insisted that "the science of political economy bears a nearer resemblance to the science of morals and politics than to that of mathematics":

> Unlike Ricardo, moreover, who wanted to calculate economic principles exclusively by mathematical deduction, Malthus continued to advocate a combination of induction and reasoning from religious principles as the best means of assessing national well-being. (Poovey, 296)

Malthus apparently lost the value debate but that has not stopped questions being asked about what we should expect markets to deliver and how we can best measure progress toward the end goal.

Rediscovering Poverty If Not Inequality

Over the years, there have been attempts to measure such ethereal concepts as quality of life and, even, happiness. Of course, not all those considered financially successful are analogously happy, and similarly, there are many happy poor people. Other measures, for example, of employment, income, productivity, and prices, are among the array of the statistical currencies accepted by economists. They are "observables."

According to Poovey, it was only with the 1832–1834 Royal Commission (well after Adam Smith's death), which was appointed to investigate the poor law, that numerical data were collected on a large enough scale to be useful for formulating—or at least defending—government policy.

Widespread poverty, a surrogate term for inequality, was certainly much discussed in America. President Franklin D. Roosevelt raised the poverty profile in his 1941 State of the Union Address by including freedom from want among his widely accepted four freedoms. The benefits of democracy, he stated, include opportunity, employment, social security, and the promise of adequate health care—all dimensions or components relevant to the general concept of enhancing equality.

All these components are studied and discussed as stand-alone challenges apparently immune from moral judgments about what is fair or not—that is, to inequality in America. Policy debates have been sanitized in ways that separate the consequences of inequality from the forces that create it, whether intended or not, justified or not.

Poverty is the absence of wealth, the canary in the coal mine that should have raised questions about the heavy emphasis economists placed on aggregate wealth, not on how that wealth is distributed.

In the past, poor laws dealt with welfare and poverty as separate policy challenges considered independently of the system that produced often widespread and cruel poverty. Creating wealth was the principal value objective that economic policies were to encourage. That bifurcated perspective continues today.

To some critics, we have poverty because we were mistaken to believe that the universal rational economic man has a good seasoning of social virtue. The poor are poor, it is assumed, because they lack both rationality and virtue. Rationality only applies to some truckers and traders. That absence of rationality, some seem to assume, is a return to the precivilized biblical era.

Joseph Schumpeter wrote that members of the working class were culturally unsuited to savings, to the creation of capital. Members of the "industrial family" were "trained to save." Workers could not be trusted to possess the same farsightedness as members of the bourgeois.[7] Only the capitalists were rational economic men, the base for modern wealth-growing economies. Schui concluded from his review of economists' writings that some number of them concluded that "only a small share of the population was intellectually and morally equipped to become frigid entrepreneurs. The remaining majority was composed of promiscuous proletarians."[8] Inequality was the price society paid for additions to wealth that benefitted all but some much more than others. This was a bell-shaped curve explanation and justification for inequality. "Hayek defended inequality as a price for liberty."[9] The price was much higher for some than for others. And some had much more liberty than others. We are back in beehives where the drones have a duty to support the queen.

That is, if everyone was the same universal economic man, then there should be shared wealth, not a skewed distribution of it. "Natural liberty" gives everyone an equal chance to accumulate wealth. The system was in place, so according to many critics, the fault lies not in the way markets are organized but in the failures of individual economic men—even if a large proportion of the citizenry fails in the race for riches. Blame the victim.

Lessons Learned

At least two general lessons are taken from this brief overview. First, early writers and those who followed them differed in their assumptions about the valued ends of society and some of the major forces that drive the behavior of participants in markets. And, second, instead of just focusing on national wealth, attention, according to some critics, should also be given to how that wealth is distributed among truckers and traders.

That second point leads to, among other topics, the current interest in inequality (the distribution of national wealth), reasons why there are different patterns of inequality (the drivers of inequality other than the fictitious Satan and armies of jinns[10]), what might be done to encourage greater equality, and the possible implications that alternative inequality scenarios might have for additions to national wealth and the total social (and spiritual) status of those differing in their wealth status.

Another implied and very significant challenging question asks whether we really live in tight rule-enforced system where we are merely intelligent puppets,[11] some of whom are more equal than others.[12]

As indicated earlier, a number of economists and others have turned their analytical attention to understanding and criticizing inequality, especially inequality of wealth, in modern societies. The contributions of Piketty, Atkinson, and Stiglitz were mentioned earlier. And the earlier-referenced Jonathan Schlefer argued that explanations of inequality do not lie in the operations of markets alone: "[T]he notion that markets best determine the distribution of income—who earns how much—depends on the invisible-hand metaphor because, absent this metaphor, markets alone cannot determine *any* wage at all, let alone an optimal one."[13]

What then are other possible meanings and explanations of inequality?

Most if not all economists follow in Adam Smith's footsteps by focusing on material (and financial) wealth as the central measuring unit to be used to assess individual well-being. It is that meaning of wealth that provides economists entry into understanding and, yes, justifying inequality found around the world today. But there are alternatives to traditional economic think, as will be further explored in the following chapter.

Notes

1. Cesar Hidalgo quoted in John Brockman, ed., *This Idea Must Die, Scientific Theories That Are Blocking Progress* (Harper, 2015), 334.
2. Polanyi (op. cit, Chapters 9 and 10) provides a provocative history of "the discovery of society" and the "increasing number of poor" during periods of English economic stagnation and spurts of growth. "[T]he foundations of economic theory were laid down during the Speenhamland period, which made appear as a competitive market economy what actually was capitalism without a labor market." (124) Economic theories were being formulated during what appear in retrospect as frequent revisits to periods of abnormality. Polanyi's coverage of Bentham, De Foe, Robinson Crusoe, Hobbes, Malthus, and others are well worth rereading.
3. Poovey, p. 284. Anyone who, like the present author, has lived and worked for decades in some of the poorest countries of Asia, the Near East, and Africa may be excused for exploring analogous dismal thoughts. Perhaps, experiencing multiple other cultures in the languages of the locals helps an observer to transcend the cultural biases one learns during years of academic exposure to mainline social, economic, political, and philosophical theories. No, the author does not consider himself a soft or bleeding heart critic.
4. Ibid., 284.
5. Op.cit., 163.
6. Ibid, 69. And "in the wake of the Napoleonic Wars, rising poor rates made poor law reform increasingly pressing..." (295).
7. Schui, 78.
8. Ibid., 148.
9. Ibid., 194.
10. The New Testament refers to Jesus casting out evil spirits from those who were demon-possessed. Histories of the world suggest that legions of

demons survived, multiplied, and both trucked and traded. There is no apparent Federal Bureau of Investigation (FBI) file that identifies demon truckers and traders. According to daily news reports, market demons are as plentiful as virtuous traders. It is possible that one can find in the religious literature coverage of Adam Smith's imaginary world in which truckers and traders are overseen by god's invisible hand, a heavenly bliss that justifies smiting evil-doing truckers and traders. Theologians, it would seem, would see a divine force behind the Prophet Adam Smith's imaginary world overseen by god's invisible hand. Physicists refer to the god particle (the Higgs boson). I suspect that an analogous image is attractive to economists and other social scientists. Puff! Readers, are you still there?

11. The philosopher John Gray has written on puppets in the theater: Kleist argued that "paradoxical as it may seem, the puppet is free in a way no human being can manage to be, precisely because it lacks consciousness; for us to achieve the gracefulness of puppets, which 'only glance the ground, like elves,' we should have to have 'either no consciousness or an infinite amount of it' ": that is to say, we should have to be either a marionette or a god. This contention Gray takes as the starting point for and, to some extent, the focus of his brief but intricate "enquiry into human freedom." Through all of his books, from *Straw Dogs* onward, Gray reiterates the point that what we consider free thinking is really no more than a ragbag of religious remnants, what Coleridge called spilt religion, whether of the secular, Socratic kind, or the version of Christianity invented by St. Paul. "All modern philosophies in which history is seen as a process of human emancipation," Gray writes, "...are garbled versions of [the] Christian narrative, itself a garbled version of the original message of Jesus—for as Nietzsche observed, there was only one Christian, and he died on the cross." From John Banville's "The Soul of the Marionette by John Gray review—bleak, bracing and highly entertaining," *The Guardian* April 25, 2015. Creative theater directors such as Lee Breuer introduce humanized puppets along with human actors in verbal and emotional exchanges between the two versions of performers. The viewing audience has an experience different from what is seen on TV and in movies that mix humans and cartoon figures.
12. According to the quantum mechanical wave function used in physics (Heisenberg's uncertainty principle), probability replaces certainty, a view that seems widely accepted by economists as well. Probability is further enhanced when economic predictions (forecasts) are presented as high, medium, and low projections. See the earlier reference to Richard E. Neustadt and Ernest R. May, *Thinking in Time: The Uses of History for Decision Makers.*
13. Op. cit., 4.

CHAPTER 7

The Long-Standing Interest in the Meanings, Causes, and Consequences of Inequality

Abstract Economists focus on the creation of wealth rather than on how that wealth is distributed among those who create it. This orientation seems to be changing with the statistical evidence provided by Thomas Piketty and others.

Numbers carry a moral tail, one that invites questions about what is normal and what is fair. Piketty's statistical analysis focused on the "normal" component, concluding that current trends are neither normal nor desirable.

If inequality is a problem, it is not an analytical one limited to analysis by economists. In the relatively recent past of the discipline, there were institutional economists who addressed concerns that we now associate with inequality.

Noneconomists, including sociologists, have written on hierarchies, a term with both statistical and moral connotations.

Keywords Piketty • Measure • Inequality • Future of economics • Sociology • Hierarchy • Moral philosophy • Statistical evidence • Normal • Wealth • Social sciences • Humanities

Not everyone agrees with the moral implications of Thomas Piketty's interpretations of inequality. He and like-minded economists are accused of wandering off the trail of their discipline's expertise. Keep to numbers even if they are based on value decisions made by past economists.

© The Editor(s) (if applicable) and the Author(s) 2016

R.E. Mitchell, *The Language of Economics*,
DOI 10.1007/978-3-319-33981-8_7

If inequality is a problem, it is not an analytical one limited to analysis by economists only. In the relatively recent past of the discipline, there were institutional economists who addressed concerns that we now associate with inequality. And Adam Smith himself observed that politics and privilege influenced the level and distribution of the wealth of a nation.

Noneconomists, including sociologists, who have written on hierarchies in general have added their voices to what is foreordained normal, a term with both statistical and moral connotations. Future progress in better understanding not just of inequality but of markets and economies more generally may depend on lowering the protective walls separating the different social sciences and humanities from one another.

Inequality Is Both a Descriptive and a Value-Laden Word

The meanings and consequences of inequality within markets and society more generally have been a continuing concern of philosophers and social analysts, including economists. For example, see Michael J. Sandel's two books *Justice, What's the Right Thing to Do*[1] and *What Money Can't Buy, The Moral Limits of Markets.*[2] He and others give due credit to John Rawls' search for principles of distributive justice based on a hypothetical initial (childhood) situation of equality under a veil of ignorance that essentially blinds people to all facts about themselves so they cannot tailor principles to their own advantage.[3] Choices made under these hypothetical conditions would strongly favor greater equality, according to Rawls.

Adam Smith focused on the creation of both aggregate and personal wealth, not on how that wealth was distributed among those who created it.

Inequality is a politically sensitive topic and issue in America today, although in earlier years, there was more open debate about differences between the multiple forms of capitalism and markets, competing schools of democratic socialism, authoritarian communist and state capitalist states, as well as the multiple meanings of "class." Many would no doubt accept that inequality does, yes, exist and that some inequality might be normal. At the same time, criticisms are being made that our current patterns of inequality are far from "normal" and that these patterns have an adverse effect on a country's ability to add to its national wealth that is distributed in a "fair" way, whatever fair (or normal) might mean.

Economists and many others are inclined to view inequality in narrow economic (monetary and wealth) terms that are beyond the expected normal, a word that is seldom assigned reasonable meaning. The traditional focus of economists since Adam Smith has been on the creation of wealth, not on how wealth is distributed. Still, distribution is something that can be statistically measured—for example, by the Gini coefficient, Palma ratio, and both the Theil and Atkinson indexes. Thomas Piketty found fault with all these measures. Instead, he relied on various configurations of statistical distribution tables. His long 685-page book and its Part Three section titled "The Statistics of Inequality" is this chapter's entry into income and wealth inequality, reasons why there has been a trend toward greater inequality, and some of the prospects for a "fairer" economic system in the future.

This chapter is organized in eight related subsections that move from Piketty's recent contributions through to other works by both economists and other social scientists who recognize that "inequality" has both statistical and value-based meanings. Both are socially constructed meanings:

1. Piketty's well-received historical review of international differences in "economic" inequality over time. Our focus is limited to the American experience.
2. How selected other economists, historians, and social scientists have viewed inequality.
3. Claims made by moral philosophers and social scientists that some patterns of inequality are neither natural nor necessary. They are results of policy choices that have been made in the past.
4. Shifting from moral values and economics, we look at the ways that some analysts have understood how politics, policies, and power have influenced the patterns and consequences of inequality.
5. Inequality, according to some observers, is to be celebrated, not criticized. We look at some of these apologies and apologists.
6. How the founding father of modern economics, Adam Smith, viewed the forces behind the inequality of his own time.
7. The focus shifts from economists to other social scientists who addressed the origins and meanings of inequality.
8. Based on the above, we close with questions that our contemporary economists and others are asking about inequality and the future of economics.

That is a lot of ground to cover in a short chapter. It also justifies this roadmap to help readers follow the story line.

Piketty's Historical Statistical Profile of American Inequality

Piketty begins his analysis by distinguishing between two different but related bases of economic inequality, one income from labor, the other income from capital. The profiles (hierarchies) of the two distributions are not the same. "The top 10 percent or bottom 50 percent of the labor income distribution are not the same 'people' who constitute the top 10 percent and bottom 50 percent of the wealth distribution." (page 254)

America's growing inequality of income is partially attributable to the rise of "super salaries." Some apologists try to justify these salaries by the old saw of increased "marginal productivity," an "ideological construct" not supported by evidence. And the same goes for new technologies employed by what Piketty labels "super managers." There is much ideology but little acceptable confirming evidence.

Capital and the income from it are more unequally distributed than income from labor. One Federal Reserve study discovered that "the top decile own 72 percent of America's wealth, while the bottom half claim just 2 percent." (page 257)

Piketty discovered an "explosive" growth of capital income, again income that is not the same as income from labor. Moreover, the return on capital is greater than the rate of growth in the economy more generally. This American trend, according to Piketty, is returning America to the dynastic type of wealth associated with earlier centuries of European economies.

The trend in how wealth and income are distributed has an adverse effect on the growth of the total national wealth. This is because, as Piketty and other economists have argued, lower-income families are losing their purchasing power. Total "demand" is throttled.

Economists and other number crunchers can describe America's return to the patrimonial capitalism of the past but they are not able to explain why the adverse trends are set in motion in the first place—that is, the most powerful forces behind America's growing inequality.

Promising explanations, he suggests, can be found in institutions. His section on "The Role of Institutions" gives special attention to the rules that govern the operation of labor markets.

Reflecting our earlier coverage of the language of economics, Piketty notes that the "labor market" is "a social construct based on specific rules and compromises," a way of thinking parallel to what earlier chapters explored. Moreover, there are cultural differences as well: the rise of super managers seems to be primarily an Anglo-Saxon phenomenon (page 315).

Inequality in America is not just a fact but also a cultural and social construct or product, not something inherent in Alice–in-Wonderland markets imagined by Adam Smith. Moreover, as Piketty recognizes, Adam Smith's "invisible hand does not exist, any more than 'pure and perfect' competition does, and the market is always embodied in specific institutions such as corporate hierarchies and compensation committees." (page 332)

How these institutions and the cultures that support them arise and operate are questions (still unanswered) for sociologists, not just economists, to probe. "The problem of inequality is a problem for the social sciences in general, not just for one of its disciplines." (page 333). That includes history and studies of literature as well, for Piketty references inequality examples from Jane Austen, *Gone with the Wind*, and other cultural artifacts.

Yes, public policy has had significant influences on an economy's evolving profile of inequality, the performance of economies, and the wealth of a nation, not just on how that wealth is distributed among those who produce and consume it. But as Piketty and others have observed, it will be very difficult if not impossible to significantly change the shape of American inequality. That is because the economically powerful have an outsized influence on policies that allow the trends toward an increasingly "hyper patrimonial" system.

Although Piketty calls for analytical contributions from other social scientists, he is silent on what these "others" might provide. His negative observation on the work and assumptions of Talcott Parsons, a leading sociologist in the mid-1900s, suggests that this discipline, like economics, must do more to escape the prison of its own socially constructed understanding of society. But there is some promise of what needs to be reinvented. It includes recognition that "real democracy" and "social justice" involve more than just "parliaments and other formal democratic institutions" (page 424).

Social scientists, including sociologists, have, of course, explored the meanings and origins of inequalities (such as "class") through their own socially constructed languages. But it is not clear what these social sciences can contribute to our understanding of inequality over and above what some economists have already observed. Adam Smith, as noted, recognized that nonmarket forces influence how wealth is distributed among truckers and traders. That is, the benefits of market transactions are not necessarily market determined. However, both economists and other social scientists seem to have accepted the view that additions to national wealth is the standard for determining how well the overall economy is doing. Total wealth is the metric for measuring "progress." At the same time, these other social sciences recognize the not-so-hidden hand of dominant "classes." So the gap between the rich and the rest is not to be explained only by normal market forces but by how power within societies is distributed.

In the real world, there is no real social contract. That is a fig leaf to justify an unequal distribution of wealth, prestige, and influence. However, study after study has documented that neither merit nor initiative is equally distributed throughout a population, so the rewards of merit and initiative (or lack of them) should not be equally distributed either. Winners, according to some political theorists, include many undeserving capitalists (those living on inherited capital wealth).

And one gets the impression that social scientists recognize that certain forms of capitalism work much better than what command economies are able to produce. But the critics also seem to agree with Adam Smith, "much more an admirer of capitalism than of capitalists."[4]

How Some Other Economists, Historians, and Social Scientists Viewed Inequality

Piketty provided necessary statistical evidence but his story is not new. Nor are his statistics the last word. New evidence continues to become available.

Let us begin with the term "capitalist." It can mask significant differences among those who contribute to economic growth.

As the previous footnote to Kevin Phillips indicated, a sizeable proportion of America's wealthiest are trust-fund babies who inherited their privileges. More recent US Department of Labor studies confirm Phillips' earlier findings as well as those of Piketty. He is not the only researcher to examine inequality.

In their 2011 US Department of Labor study, Edward N. Wolff and Maury Gittleman, for example, found that

> "inheritances and gifts have historically accounted for between 20 and 50 percent of total household wealth accumulation in the U.S. Wealth transfers are also an important source of both business and home ownership." The wealthiest 1 percent of families had inherited an average of $2.7 million from their parents. This was 447 times more money than the least wealthy group of people—those with wealth less than $25K—had inherited. In between the wealthiest and least wealthy groups, inheritance levels ran in exactly the direction you would expect: the wealthier a group of people was, the more they had inherited.[5]

A year later, in 2012, *Fortune* magazine reported that "[t]he vast majority of millionaires inherited their wealth or built it on a business they founded."[6] The privileged status of many of the inheritors, those families that Phillips listed in his study, cannot be easily justified as normal inequality, something that resulted from an individual's contribution of adding wealth to the nation.

For this and many other reasons, it is not surprising that some critics have argued that our current distribution of wealth and associated privileges are neither normal nor a result of the perfect markets that Adam Smith imagined. Piketty was essentially correct in his research findings. And other studies seem to suggest that some forms and patterns of distributions can impede an economy from adding to its wealth, an addition that could better benefit all those who contribute to the creation of wealth. Inequality can be antigrowth.

Reducing inequality might, however, require a new social contract and means to enforce it.

This new attention to inequality again turns our attention to how and who "invents" and "authors" history and economic textbooks, and gives meanings to terms such as "progress" and "inequality." Yes, we live under a politically protected moral and economic catechism, but earlier catechisms were sometimes replaced to the benefit of the broad public. That was one of the challenges of the Enlightenment (and Franklin D. Roosevelt's New Deal). Perhaps, the attention that has recently been given to inequality will also lift the veil of conformity represented by economists and those who most benefit from all forms of contemporary inequality.

Not all economists, of course, believe their discipline has the key to understanding "what determines the distribution of income in a society," for this is a question within "the domain of grand theories," and "universal theories are impossible to formulate in the social sciences." Economists, however, are able to address such questions as why inequality has increased so much in the USA since the 1970s. Even then, no single theory, according to Rodrik, can "fully" explain these changes.[7]

Moral Philosophy: Some Inequality Is Neither Natural Nor Necessary

Whether they are aware of it or not, economists today who use the term "inequality" are returning to moral philosophy, a field the economics discipline abandoned on its way to political economy, and then just to economics as the domain of their expertise. But the descriptive language of the discipline can and has masked alternative ways that markets might be organized to spread the benefits of growth for all without sacrificing increases in total national wealth. In fact, it might be argued, as already done above, that the way wealth is currently distributed not only harms a vast majority of income earners but also inhibits an economy from realizing its full aggregate wealth potential.

Both Joseph Stiglitz in his previously referenced writings on inequality and Monica Prasad in her pathbreaking *The Land of Too Much*[8] demonstrate that ***inequality is a policy choice***, although the consequences arising from choices were not necessarily understood at the time they were made.

Prasad begins her award-winning book with the following:

> One of the central questions of comparative political economy is why there is so much more poverty [and inequality] in the United States than in any other developed country. In any way that we can measure poverty, the United States fares worse than other countries, even if we control for factors such as the different racial composition and immigration history of the American population.

And empirical studies have shown that "even when we use absolute rather than relative measures of poverty, the United States remains near the top of the list of advanced countries with the highest poverty."

Prasad also corrects the misperception that the European countries that have been more successful in alleviating the pains of poverty did so by favoring consumer interests over those of the private sector. That claim is simply based on ignorance and/or self-serving ideology, as Prasad documents throughout her book.

Contrary to popular American assumptions, according to Prasad, European governments have fewer restrictions on markets than what exists in America. And the same generality applies to taxes, for it is not tax rates that distinguish America from European countries but, instead, the difference is found in what is taxed by whom as well as how tax revenues are used to address a country's multiple needs, including those that might alleviate the results attributable to inequality.

One needs to read Prasad for how she combines economic, political, sociological, and historical sources to understand why America has public welfare for the well-off and weak private welfare for the less fortunate.

The Role of Politics, Policy, and Power

Many would no doubt agree with Prasad's and Piketty's conclusion that the "fundamental cause of poverty is political" and that America has socialism for the rich. The USA does have high tax rates on corporations but then offers major exceptions through the backdoor of tax preferences.

How did all this happen? According to Prasad, there was a "curious process by which agricultural overproduction led to a focus on tax progressivity, which in turn constrained the welfare state." (171).

The Land of Too Much must be read in the original, not in my snippets of quotations. Her conclusions reinforce those of Stiglitz and others that inequality as we know it is a *policy choice*. And Prasad reminds us that we have a "socially constructed" map of the "nature of the economic world." (145) The same applies to the various meanings assigned to inequality. Again, the distribution of wealth and the portrait of inequality are the consequences of public policies, whether intentionally formulated or not. There has never been an invisible hand behind the formulation of inequality policies. The distribution of wealth and the distribution of influence and power are mutually interdependent in not-so-invisible ways.

There is nothing new in this observation, for it has a long historical tradition in America. My *A Concise History* references some of the past critics of American markets, inequalities, and proposed reform agendas. Rhetorical battles continue today between those holding different mental models of the links between economic and sociopolitical systems and policies. Economies are imbedded in larger social, cultural, and political systems that tend to reinforce one another.

Change is obviously difficult—but not necessarily impossible. It may well require recognition that some (not all) of our inherited mental models are dangerous fictions. The world moves on, as it did soon after Adam Smith published his *The Wealth of Nations*. Some economists and others are still anchored in the far past.

But let us recognize again that *inequality* as well are *equality* are value-laden terms, just as are so many words in the dictionaries of contemporary economics and public life more generally.

Apologists for Inequality

Economists, including Stiglitz, assume that a certain amount of inequality encourages risk-taking that, in an economy where private property is protected, continually propels the economy toward higher and higher levels of wealth creation that benefits all.

Free-market fundamentalists seem to prefer the value-laden term *meritocracy* to justify value-laden *inequality*. Piketty refers to arguments that assume we live in a "hypermeritocractic society" with "supermanagers" and "superstars." Those who use their brains backed by energy and initiative should be rewarded, as they obviously are. But economists such as Adam Smith and David Ricardo observed that England's large landowning aristocracy passed their wealth down through the generations, thereby relieving the inheritors of having to make their own contributions. They did not with their own initiative create the wealth they controlled.

Well before Piketty, Kevin Phillips and others documented that America has its own aristocracy of wealth and patrimonial capitalism, with those at the top of the wealth pyramid living off of what they inherited rather than from their own contribution to the wealth of the nation.[9] Of course, there are many self-made millionaires who did not build their fortunes on what they inherited from their ancestors.

Still, the apologists' fig leaf of meritocracy has its ideological limits.

That's Not How Adam Smith Saw It

Social, political, economic, and religious inequality over the ages cannot be justified by the assumed meritocracy claim. Inequality (aka the distribution of power [influence], prestige, wealth, and more) is a socially and culturally imbedded reality that extends well beyond economies and markets. Early institutional economists and others recognized this. Marx, Veblen, John Commons' *Legal Foundations of Capitalism* (1924), John Kenneth Galbraith's *Countervailing Power* (1952) and *The New Industrial State* (1967), along with many others no longer well represented in academic departments of economics, vainly argued that markets are not *sui generis* but can only be understood when placed in a larger social and cultural context. Adam Smith, as noted, also was aware of this, as he wrote:

> People of the same trade seldom meet together, even for merriment and diversion, but the conversation ends in a conspiracy against the public, or in some contrivance to raise prices. It is impossible indeed to prevent such meetings, by any law which either could be executed, or would be consistent with liberty and justice. But though the law cannot hinder people of the same trade from sometimes assembling together, it ought to do nothing to facilitate such assemblies; much less to render them necessary. (*Wealth of Nations* 1.10.82).

> To expect, indeed, that the freedom of trade should ever be entirely restored in Great Britain is as absurd as to expect that an Oceana or Utopia should ever be established in it. Not only the prejudices of the public, but what is much more unconquerable, the private interests of many individuals, irresistibly oppose it. (IV.2.43)
>
> The legislature, were it possible that its deliberations could be always directed, not by the clamorous importunity of partial interests, but by an extensive view of the general good, ought upon this very account, perhaps, to be particularly careful neither to establish any new monopolies of this kind, nor to extend further those which are already established. Every such regulation introduces some degree of real disorder into the constitution of the state, which it will be difficult afterwards to cure without occasioning another disorder. (IV.2.44)

Smith provided numerous examples of how governments distort markets. For example,

> Civil government supposes certain subordination. But as the necessity of civil government gradually grows up with the acquisition of valuable property, so the principal causes which naturally introduce subordination gradually grow up with the growth of that valuable property. (V.1. 46)
>
> Civil government, so far as it is instituted for the security of property, is in reality instituted for the defence of the rich against the poor, or of those who have some property against those who have none at all. (V.1. 55)

Government, according to Smith, can have a potential countervailing role in restraining the inequities introduced by a class system:

> *[E]xertions of the natural liberty of a few individuals, which might endanger the security of the whole society, are, and ought to be, restrained by the laws of all governments, of the most free as well as of the most despotical.* (V1.2.393, emphasis added. He references "individuals," not "governments," as the culprits.)

Keynes as well was critical of the concept of natural liberty, a concept implicit in Adam Smith's legacy and one still central to various advocacy centers. I will repeat an earlier reference that Keynes made about:

> the metaphysical or general principles upon which, from time to time, laissez-faire has been founded. It is not true that individuals possess a prescriptive "natural liberty" in their economic activities. There is no

> "compact" conferring perpetual rights on those who Have or on those who Acquire. The world is not so governed from above that private and social interest always coincide.

To some purists and model-builders, today's economics profession has become a cacophony of terms and concepts still based on an outdated dictionary invented for earlier times, not the world we have today. Yet this is the language that students of economics inherit from their elders, thereby perpetuating the myths and mistakes of the past.

Michels, Weber, and Other Social Scientists

There are multiple relevant pasts that economists might be advised to revisit. For example, the German sociologist Robert Michels claimed in his 1911 book *Political Parties: A Sociological Study of the Oligarchical Tendencies of Modern Democracy Political Parties*[10] that rule by an elite, or oligarchy, is an inevitable "iron law" within any democratic organization as part of the "tactical and technical necessities" of organization. But that does not justify high levels of wealth and income inequality, at least according to Prasad as well as Joseph Stiglitz. The latter agrees with Piketty and Prasad that "the level of inequality in America is not inevitable; it is not the result of inexorable laws of economics. It is a matter of policies and politics."[11]

Others would suggest that inequality is just one of many manifestations of a more general reality of "hierarchies." Bourdieu, for example, described hierarchies in cultural production, not in markets per se.[12]

Still other specialists in organizations have equated hierarchies with the chain of command that allows for greater (or less) success.

But the general concept of hierarchy and the inequality component within it do not provide nor suggest criteria for assessing alternative hierarchical profiles (profiles in the plural). This suggests that how markets distribute wealth and income should be placed within a larger context of how power and influence are distributed (other hierarchy profiles). That returns the focus to political economy, not just to narrow economics.

But a note of caution, for according to some economists, Stiglitz and Piketty are wandering off the central interests and competencies of the economics discipline. The Nobel Prize winner Robert Lucas, for example, claimed:

> Of the tendencies that are harmful to sound economics, the most seductive and...poisonous is to focus on questions of distribution...[moreover]

> Of the vast increase in the well-being of hundreds of millions of people that has occurred in the 200-year course of the industrial revolution to date, virtually none of it can be attributed to the direct redistribution of resources from rich to poor. The potential for improving the lives of poor people by finding different ways of distributing current production is *nothing* compared to the apparently limitless potential of increasing production.[13]

Lucas, of course, is not the only economist who believes that their discipline should focus on the size of the economic pie, not on how it is divided. According to Stiglitz:

> There is in fact a long tradition in economics that holds that the two issues (of efficiency and distribution, of the size of the pie and how it is divided) can be separated, and that the job of the economist was narrow, important: it was only to figure out how to maximize the size of the pie. The division of the pie was a matter of politics, something that economists should stay well clear of.[14]

As they have.

I do not think that the critics of American inequality are referring only to the redistribution of rewards but also to the rules of the political game that define how rewards are to be allocated in the first place. Political power influences how wealth is distributed, or as Stiglitz claimed, inequalities we now have in America are "not inevitable, the inexorable workings out of the laws of economics: rather they were the results of our policies and politics."[15]

This is not a new finding or claim. Well before Piketty, Deaton, Prasad, and Stiglitz, generations of institutional economists made the same point, although this school within the discipline has largely disappeared. The institutionalists and other critics claimed that the drivers of markets and economies are not to be found only within markets themselves but also from influences exogenous to them. Wealth inequality is coterminous with and dependent on political inequality. The yin and yang of wealth and influence overlap and reinforce one another. (I cover the differences between endogenous and exogenous influences on markets in my *A Concise History of Economist's Assumptions About Markets.*)

In his *Great Escape*, Deaton considers both inter- and intranational differences in how innovations in public health and medicine drove changes in individual well-being as well as patterns of unequal well-being. He goes well beyond narrow economics in his analysis of the drivers of inequality. In doing this, he identifies some of the questionable value assumptions that economists make. For example, Pareto's optimality claim is limited to "income," whereas well-being has broader meanings. And the economist's focus on equality of opportunity fails to consider equality of outcomes. Well-being has many dimensions beyond the economist's narrow focus on money (whether from earned income or from wealth). Economists are trapped in the value assumptions of their discipline (and rewarded by the Nobel Prize selection committee).

The German sociologist Max Weber (like Michels) also saw unequal power as an inherent feature of bureaucracies and, by extension, of societies more generally. Inequality is essential to the decision-making process, one that rewards those with the most power. And the Italian engineer and economist Vilfredo Pareto proposed the law of the vital few, or the 80-20 rule based on the principle of factor sparsity, in which for many events, roughly 80% of the effects come from 20% of the causes.[16]

Whether or not meritocracy and Pareto's rule justify inequality, inequality seems to be a fact of life, a challenge for economists and others, who in making policy recommendations will often propose changes (or reinforcement of) to the current distribution of economic and noneconomic resources, benefits, and power.

But what happens in markets does not necessarily stay in markets.

There are spillover effects on the larger social and political power systems. These systems, it seems, are not independent of one another. Perhaps, that is one reason that helps explain the rise of university policy centers that require students to become semiproficient in multiple traditional academic disciplines, not just economics.[17]

A review of the contributions made by the institutional economist Robert North captures some of what we have already covered to this point. According to one of the obituaries of this inventive scholar:

> [W]e must have more than a history of markets to understand economic change...[for] the presence of transactions costs, political systems do not inevitably evolve institutions that promote economic growth...the tendency is for political systems to evolve that do not support growth...we need a theory of organizations as well as a theory of beliefs and ideology if we are to understand long run change, particularly long run change that does not inevitably produce growth and development.

The reviewer noted that economists inherit:

beliefs [including facts, images, values, paradigms and theories that] are always a function of what happened in the past and can impede change in the present for good or ill. It is the persistence of beliefs and institutions from the past (culture) that explain why changes in the present often produce results that impede rather than promoting growth and development.

North placed economic history within an institutional context:

Institutions, which regularly emphasizes that the function of an institution is to provide stability and predictability to human behavior...Institutions are the rules of the game and the means of enforcement, and organizations are the teams that play the game.

Robert North's fourth major contribution, according to his biographer, was to separate institutions and organizations.[18]

Questions Economists and Others Are Asking

Some economists fault their colleagues for their misguided assumptions and theories that, if corrected, could help us better understand markets and the unequal effects they presumably now produce. According to Stiglitz (among others): "Economists provided models—based on unrealistic assumptions of perfect information, perfect competition, and perfect markets—in which regulation was not necessary."[19] More realistic fact-based assumptions are needed in the models that economists and others construct.

There could hopefully be some positive crossover spillage effects from an interdisciplinary (or nondisciplinary) approach to understanding inequality and how to change it. Central to this crossover is the recognition, as Lawrence Freedman noted in another connection, that "theories of strategy that lacked a theory of power are bound to mislead."[20]

Power, like wealth, is distributed within a society and overlaps a country's profile of inequality. In a theoretically equal society, one man, one vote would be the mantra, not one dollar, one vote, an oft-quoted description of contemporary America.

Piketty seems to be an exception, whereas his fellow economists appear to be overly protective of their king-like status with no trespassing signs warning other social scientists to keep away from markets and the processes within them. Paul Krugman reported this bias among some of his fellow economists as follows:

> An Indian-born economist once explained his personal theory of reincarnation to his graduate economics class: "If you are a good economist, a virtuous economist," he said, "you are reborn as a physicist. But if you are an evil, wicked economist, you are reborn a sociologist."

Krugman went on to note: "Economics is *harder* than physics; luckily it is not quite as hard as sociology."[21]

History professor Ian Morris looked far back in time to link changing patterns of inequality to earlier economic theories and biases. In his *New York Times* contribution, he asked:

> How much inequality is too much? Is it possible for there to be too little inequality? And, most important, is there a "right" amount of inequality?
>
> [E]ach age has gotten the inequality it needs, different economic systems functioning best with different levels of inequality. Down through the centuries, groups that have moved toward the most effective amount of inequality reaped benefits; those that did not paid a price.
>
> Anthropological studies of foraging societies suggest that their Gini coefficients for income and accumulated wealth both averaged around 0.25. In farming societies, however, the average income inequality almost doubled, to 0.45. The Roman Empire scored around 0.43, England in 1688 about 0.47, and France on the eve of the Revolution an eye-watering 0.59. Inequality in accumulated wealth increased even more, regularly topping 0.80.[22]

Statistical norms, of course, are not moral ones (at least they need not be). Life in the past could, as Hobbs wrote, be nasty, brutish, and short. Alternative patterns of inequality might have better advantaged all. Statistics do not justify the patterns they reveal. Still, how much inequality is too much and why is "too much" something to avoid?

Inequality (or descriptively equivalent terms relating to the distribution of wealth and, yes, power) is certainly not new. Economists have been measuring it, but until Piketty and a few others, there was little consensus on how to explain various inequality patterns or whether it should be discussed at all.

Finally, two decades ago, in 1994, Paul Krugman wrote: "For the most remarkable thing about the debate over growing inequality in the USA has been the reluctance of many conservatives to admit it happened at all":

> Conservative denial of the reality of the growth of inequality in the United States has taken three main forms. The first is to question the numbers; the second is to dismiss the distributional question as irrelevant in the face of a supposed growth triumph; the third is to argue that income distribution is irrelevant in a society with high social mobility.[23]

At the same time, Krugman remarked that "while we can make some interesting speculations, we really don't know very well why inequality has increased. That does not mean that nothing can be done about it." (p. 150) Again, he wrote that more than two decades before Piketty (before Deaton, a fellow Princeton economist).

Since Krugman wrote that in 1994, Piketty, Atkinson, Stiglitz, Deaton, Prasad, and others provided information on the status of inequality and its plausible causes. According to Stiglitz, we now have what he and others label ersatz, phony capitalism, corporate welfare, and socialism for the rich. "We don't have a truly competitive economy." Those who succeed too often pull up the ladder they climbed to the top.

Through political power, those with the most wealth have created barriers to competition. Adam Smith also saw this same game, as did the reformers in America's Gilded Age, the setting for Lizzie Magie's invention of the still popular "The Landlord's Game," now known as Monopoly.[24] The result today is suggested by the title of one of Stiglitz's chapters: In No One We Trust.

Yes, Stiglitz and others recognize that some inequality may be necessary to encourage thrift, innovation, risk-taking, and industry.[25] But the level of inequality we now have is not inevitable nor the kind of economy that would best add to the wealth of a nation and the welfare of all.

Economists and others continue to grapple with the challenge of understanding inequality independently of the moral overtones of this socially constructed term in the vocabulary of the social sciences.[26]

Notes

1. Farrar, Straus and Giroux, 2009.
2. Farrar, Straus and Giroux, 2012.
3. Rawls, *A Theory of Justice* (Belknap, 1971).
4. Schui, 53.
5. Bureau of Labor Statistics January 2011 report, *Inheritances and the Distribution of Wealth or Whatever Happened to the Great Inheritance Boom?* Available online at http://www.bls.gov/ore/pdf/ec110030.pdf.

6. Carol J Loomis, "Should you leave it all to the children?" *Fortune*, November 21, 2012. There are, of course, self-made millionaires as well.
7. Rodrik, op. cit., 116, 121, 143.
8. Harvard, 2012. For a critical review of Prasad's and other recent sociological studies of contemporary American political economy, see Jeff Manza's "Reconnecting the Political and the Economic in the New Gilded Age," *Contemporary Sociology* (July 2015).
9. Kevin Phillips, *Wealth and Democracy: A Political History of the American Rich* (Broadway 2003).
10. Robert Michels, *Political Parties: A Sociological Study of the Oligarchical Tendencies of Modern Democracy Political Parties* (1911). "Oligarchy" has a long history that includes Socrates in Plato's *Republic*: "*How does the change from oligarchy into democracy arise?*"
11. *The Great Divide*, xii.
12. Pierre Bourdieu, "The Field of Cultural Production, or: The Economic World Reversed," reprinted in Craig Calhoun et al, eds., *Contemporary Sociological Theory* (Blackwell, 2007).
13. Robert Lucas, "The Industrial Revolution: Past and Present," 2003 Annual Report Essay, Federal Reserve Bank of Minneapolis, May 1, 2014. Reported in Stiglitz, xxv.
14. Ibid., xv.
15. In writing short popular articles for noneconomists (as well as his fellow members of that discipline), Stiglitz did not have sufficient space to provide the detailed evidence in support of his arguments.
16. Twenty percent of American health-care patients are estimated to be using 80% of health-care resources. Some criminology studies discovered that 80% of crimes are committed by 20% of criminals. This ratio is known as profit risk in the financial services industry, where 20% or fewer of a company's customers are generating positive income, while 80% or more are costing the company money. These are statistical regularities devoid of explanation and assumed causation. Piketty is critical of Pareto's law of "stable inequality and the pointlessness of trying to change it," as well as Pareto's "powers law," as it only applies to the upper tail of distributions and the relation is only approximate and locally valid. See his discussion on page 367.
17. When the author graduated from Harvard's China Area Program under John King Fairbanks in 1955, the excellent faculty focused more on what to think rather than how to think. Harvard's current Kennedy School of Government, along with sister programs in other universities, offers students with classes in several disciplines that cover how, not just what, to think. There has been change for the better.
18. Obituary: Douglass C. North, EH.net Nov 11/25/15.
19. Op. cit., 54. Rodrik is worth reading for his critical coverage of the limits and uses of models.

20. Freedman, op. cit., 557.
21. *Peddling Prosperity*, xi.
22. Ian Morris, "To Each Age Its Inequality," *New York Times Opinion Pages*, July 9, 2015. For an anthropological perspective on the economics of certain tribal societies, see Marshall Sahlins' *Stone Age Economics* (Aldine Transaction, 1974).
23. *Peddling Prosperity*, 130.
24. For more background on the Gilded Age, Henry George, Mark Twain, and others, see the author's *A Concise History*. George (1839–1897) offered in his *Progress and Poverty* (1879) a solution (the single tax on land) to remedy American inequality and continuing market cycles. He argued that people should own what they create but that the value of land, like nature itself, belongs to all of humanity. But both land and unearned wealth were becoming increasingly concentrated in America, a trend that he saw was creating a system of wage slavery and that later economists would extend into theories of rentier income and the rentier state. George argued that his proposed land value tax would help end inequality and the ever-destructive business cycles suffered in the American economy. His book sold over 3 million copies.
25. Recent studies of patents suggest that instead of promoting innovations, they are a drag on the economy. See "Intellectual Property: A Question of Utility," *The Economist* (August 8–14, 2015). An earlier reference was made to the contributions of organizational innovations that presumably are not patentable.
26. Rodrik (214) notes that economists use the yardstick of "efficiency" to assess the benefits that presumably result from the ways markets are organized. Along with Malthus, he is clear that "efficiency" is not everything.

CHAPTER 8

Is the Past a Reliable Prologue for the Future of Economics?

Abstract Is economics becoming irrelevant?

Other social sciences are beginning to invade the economists' territory with alternatives and supplements..

Certainly, the discipline's success in predicting the future has not been uniformly stellar. Still, there is much that the discipline has to offer. Perhaps future progress will come easier if the discipline can abandon its not-so-hidden value assumptions and disassociate itself from the well-funded "think tanks" that are so heavily committed to "old think."

This will not be easy for instead of other social sciences impinging on the turf of economists, the reverse flow continues as ways of thinking like an economist persist to colonize the other social sciences.

Keywords Social learning • Hyperconnected • Laws of economics • Human behavior • Institutions • Master system • Creativity • Innovation • Ideology • Think tanks

The house of economics is inhabited by very bright numerically adept PhDs. But is the discipline in a rut of irrelevance, one that Alfred Marshall set in motion when he expunged the term "political" from the title of his academic department?

Some economists have begun to question the foundation of their discipline and its ideological baggage.

© The Editor(s) (if applicable) and the Author(s) 2016

R.E. Mitchell, *The Language of Economics*,
DOI 10.1007/978-3-319-33981-8_8

And members of other social sciences are beginning to invade the territory that economists have attempted to wall off for themselves only. There are both alternatives and supplements to economics on the horizon.

Economists are no doubt aware that their discipline will continue to be criticized and even ignored. Certainly, the discipline's success in predicting the future has not been uniformly stellar. Still, there is much that the discipline has to offer.

Perhaps future progress will come easier if the discipline can abandon its not-so-hidden value assumptions and disassociate itself from the well-funded "think tanks" that are so heavily committed to "old think."

This won't be easy, for instead of other social sciences impinging on the turf of economists, the reverse flow continues as ways of thinking like an economist persist to colonize the other social sciences.

The subtitle for this historical review that you have been reading is *How, What, and Why Economists Think They Know What They Know: The Biased Hand of Old Socially Constructed Vocabularies.*

Over time, metaphors and conjectures used by economists have become increasingly anchored in facts that are subject to standard statistical and mathematical manipulation. Economists are certified experts, and in fact, they and their thousands of publications based on facts interpreted within now-standard mental models have added to our understanding (and confusion) of how markets and economies operate as well as how in theory they should operate if specific policy changes could be implemented.

But as the oft-mentioned distinction between Freshwater and Saltwater economists suggests, as well as the cemetery of recently claimed truths (analyzed by Paul Krugman in his *Peddling Prosperity*), this discipline does not rest on the same consensus found among the hard sciences. Perhaps this is partially explained by the very nature of societies and economies. The physical world seems to have a coherent unity that is lacking in an ever-evolving real world of truckers and traders. Of course, economic thought and understanding may have a breakout moment.

Looking to the Future

Some economists have already asked questions about what economics textbooks and courses might be like in the unknown future.

For example, in his "Our Children's Economics" for the *Project Syndicate Blog* (February 11, 2013), Barry Eichengreen placed contemporary economic thinking in an historical context:

> The economics profession has not had a good crisis. Queen Elizabeth II may have expected too much when she famously asked why economists had failed to foresee the disaster, but there is a widespread sense that much of their research turned out to be irrelevant. Worse still, much of the advice proffered by economists was of little use to policymakers seeking to limit the economic and financial fallout.

After reviewing suggestions made by representatives of several subspecialties within the discipline, Eichengreen concluded:

> A textbook two decades from now might be more sophisticated than this year's edition, fully integrating contributions that today constitute the frontiers of economic research. But it would not differ fundamentally in structure or approach from today's economics.
>
> The consensus, in other words, seemed to be that there would be nothing in the next 20 years as transformative as Alfred Marshall's synthesis of the 1890's or the revolution initiated by John Maynard Keynes in the 1930's. In contrast to the economics of those years, economics today is a mature, well-established discipline. And, like any mature discipline, it advances incrementally rather than in revolutionary steps.
>
> This presumption is almost certainly mistaken. It reflects the same error made by scholars of technology who argue that all of the radical breakthroughs have already been made…
>
> [W]e can't say what the next revolution in economic analysis will be, but more than a century of modern economic thinking suggests that there will be one.
>
> All of this suggests that the economics textbook of 2033 will look very different from the economics textbook of today. We just can't say how.

One would hope so.

Lawless Laws

Over the decades, economists formulated a number of basic laws as well as a large number of formulae such as demand function, income elasticity, measures of sustainable growth, and a great number of others. Basic laws, however, may only be ideological fictions created to help defend certain special interests. For example, Say's law or "the law of markets" is based on the claim that "[a] product is no sooner created, than it, from that instant, affords a market for other products to the full extent of its own value" and "[a]s each of us can only purchase the productions of others with his own productions—as the value we can buy is equal to the value we can produce, the more men can produce, the more they will purchase." That is, aggregate product (supply) creates an equal quantity of aggregate demand, a world in which there should be minimal business cycles.[1]

Other hypotheses, such as Okum's rule of thumb (or law), were based on empirical observations rather than a result derived from theory. The same might be said of the often-referenced IS–LM model (the Hicks–Hansen model), a "tool" used to analyze the relationship between interest rates and real output in the goods and services market and the money market (also known as the assets market).[2]

Formulae seem to be an accepted necessity for those measuring and analyzing markets. But as laws, they are much more questionable. As one critic claimed:

> [E]ven if there are laws of economics, we haven't been observing them for long enough to know what they actually are. And given the vagaries of human behavior and the mercurial nature of states, people and institutions, the notion that there's some grand mechanistic, master system that explains all and predicts everything is at best a comforting fiction and at worst a strait-jacket that precludes creativity, forestalls innovation and destroys dynamism.
>
> Referencing "the laws of economics" as a way to refute arguments or criticize ideas has the patina of clarity and certainty. The reality is that referencing such laws is simply another way to justify beliefs and inclinations.[3]

Economics may not yet be a science, but number-crunching economists certainly are adept in using scientific procedures. The same goes for political scientists and scientists of society (sociologists and anthropologists, respectively) as well as the growing number of policy analysts, some of whom are attempting to bridge the keep-out warnings of the traditional social science disciplines. We also now have an expanding array of social system analysts.

Enter the Alternatives

Alex Pentland is among an evolving new population of analysts. In his *Social Physics*,[4] he argues that the horse-and-buggy imagery and vocabulary of Adam Smith and his focus on adding to wealth fail to capture the components and processes found in our contemporary service and knowledge-based economies. "In our new hyperconnected world, most [social and economic] ties are weak, and all too often the invisible hand no longer functions." Instead of the "old vocabulary of markets and class, capital and production," economists need to recognize that people and markets move more than goods and money: the flow of information and ideas is even more important today. Instead of focusing primarily on rational thinking, one must understand how social networks (the social context abandoned by economists when political economy was replaced by eco- nomics alone) operate. Moreover,

> Standard economic incentives miss the mark because they frame people as individual, rational actors rather than as social creatures influenced by social ties.
>
> Modern society is based on the idea that markets can distribute resources efficiently and on the assumption that humans are relentless competitors. But as we have seen, this is not a good description of how our society lives and functions.[5]

Ideas associated with Adam Smith, according to some critics, have long passed their "sell-by date." Move out of the way for new vocabularies, grammars, and mental models (in the plural). To some, this has been the history of the physical sciences in its search for a theory of everything (e.g., string theory).

The social sciences, including economics, are far from the Eureka moment of everything. Many are satisfied with what Robert K. Merton called "middle-range theories":

> ...what might be called theories of the middle range: theories intermediate to the minor working hypotheses evolved in abundance during the day-by-day routine of research, and the all-inclusive speculations comprising a master conceptual scheme.
>
> Our major task today is to develop special theories applicable to limited conceptual ranges—theories, for example, of deviant behavior, the unanticipated consequences of purposive action, social perception, reference groups, social control, the interdependence of social institutions—rather than to seek the total conceptual structure that is adequate to derive these and other theories of the middle range.[6]

Pentland is hardly alone in arguing that

> [h]uman behavior is determined as much by social context as by rational thinking and individual desires. Rationality, as economists use the term,

> means that the individual knows what he or she wants and acts to get it. But this new research shows that in this regard, social network effects often, and perhaps typically dominate both the desires and the decisions of individuals…
>
> Our ability to survive and prosper is due to social learning and social influence at least as much as to individual rationality…Our desires and preferences are mostly based on what our peer community agrees is valuable, rather than on rational reflection based directly on our individual biological drives and inborn morals…In most things we're collectively rational, and only in some areas are we individually rational.[7]

The new social physics is really not so new, for it has a long history within the discipline of sociology, including the sociology of knowledge.[8] For example, Columbia University's Bureau of Applied Social Research under the initial guidance of Paul Lazarsfeld (as well as Robert K. Merton) explored the flow of political influence in national elections (the two-step flow as well as cosmopolitans and locals), consumer behavior (market research), and how social networks influence the diffusion and adoption of new prescriptions within the medical community. In my *A Concise History*, I relate this research tradition to Joseph Schumpeter's focus on change agents that include the innovators that help drive markets and economies.

With its focus on network analysis and the use of macro data, proponents of the new social physics provide an additional way to understand our ever-evolving social and economic world. Instead of asking how trucking and trading between economic agents adds to the wealth of the nation, social physics explores how the flow of information influences innovation or lack of it in societies without the strong social ties that supposedly existed in the Scotland of Adam Smith's lifetime. The new social physics requires a new dictionary to replace the "old think" of tired old economics. The proponents of this new initiative look forward to a paradigm shift.

But traditional economics still has much to contribute—for example, it is hard to see how social physics can improve on what is sometimes correctly seen to happen in financial markets. And as one economist has noted, despite the alleged limitations of certain schools of economics, there have also been adjustments and successes. For example,

> To be sure, stagflation showed that there were limits to what policy can do. But students continued to learn about the imperfections of markets and the role that monetary and fiscal policy can play in boosting a depressed economy.

And the M.I.T. students of the 1970s enlarged on those insights in their later work. Mr. Blanchard, for examples, showed how small deviations from perfect rationality can have large economic consequences; Mr. Obstfeld showed that currency markets can sometimes experience self-fulfilling panic.[9]

Caution Again

But one must temper caution, as I noted in my *A Concise History*: markets and economies are just too large and diversified with too many time-ordered nonlinear relationships among relevant intermediate variables to allow uniformly reliable predictions. Perhaps in response to these reservations, some researchers narrow their focus on relatively few variables and economic or statistical models to help explain the directions the economy is taking and what influences the pace of the changes that are being predicted. The Federal Reserve, for example, draws on several different models (not all for the same purpose).

But certainly those who make a living off of movements of markets and economies should be able to harness their understanding of how economists think to predict the future in order to make investment decisions based on their predictions. Unfortunately, some studies raise questions about these predictions, as well as the wisdom of the crowd of financial and economic forecasts currently in use. For example, Shiller recognized the poor track record of economists. After scanning newspapers' coverage of the economy, he "found virtually no warning from economists of a severe crisis ahead," the recent depression.[10]

And those sophisticated number crunchers who advise clients on how to invest their money have poor track records as well. "Back in 1995, economist and *Financial Times* columnist John Kay examined the record of 34 British forecasters from 1987 to 1994, and he concluded that they were birds of a feather. They tended to make similar forecasts, and then the economy disobligingly did something else, with economic growth usually falling outside the range of all 34 forecasters." Ten years later, "in 2005, the economy grew more slowly than 19 out of 21 forecasters had expected at the end of the previous year."[11]

Recent US forecasters have done a little better: The spread of forecasts is tighter, and the outcome sometimes falls within what is considered an acceptable spread. Still, five out of six were too pessimistic about 2003, almost everyone was too pessimistic about 2002, three-quarters were too optimistic about 2005, and nearly nine-tenths were too optimistic about

2006. Perversely, the best quantitative end-of-year forecasts were made in December 2006, despite the fact that the credit crunch materialized eight months later to the surprise of almost everybody.[12] An Ouija board could perhaps have made better predictions.

I suspect that no single school of economic thought is immune from errors of analysis and prediction. This suggests that errors in managing an economy are likely as well. That does not mean, however, that all schools of thought are equally off the mark. Krugman's *Peddling Prosperity* covers some of the more erroneous theories and predictions claimed by some certified economists. (Economists can be a contentious lot, suggesting that caveat emptor is an appropriate filter to use when digesting economic analyses and policy prescriptions.)

Asking Other Questions

Perhaps the new and old approaches are asking different questions using different languages (science speak). But these markets and their multiple social components bridge multiple disciplinary approaches from economic sociology to political systems to institutional and behavioral economics, each with their own sometimes-questionable assumptions, metaphors, conjectures, hidden values, and mental models. I doubt that a single comprehensive unified mental model of markets and economies is in the foreseeable future. We are left, then, with naysayers, question raisers, critics, and authors of books about the epistemological history of the economics discipline.

You have just completed a partial reflection of how these multiple communities understand markets, their key components, and theories about what drives them. Although a long road lies ahead, "a journey of a thousand miles begins with a single step; even the longest and most difficult ventures have a starting point." (Lao Tzu in the *Tao Te Ching*.) Centuries of earlier travelers unfortunately left trails to dead ends.

Before closing, let us look back and again ask how important rational economic man is to the discipline of economics. If such a man never existed, would we still have rational markets? Must rational markets necessarily assume that there are rational economic men? And if markets do not act rationally, does that raise questions about the necessity of assuming that there is a rational economic man?

The socially constructed concept of a rational economic man has been combined with a socially constructed imaginary invisible hand that itself makes sure that rational principles are adopted (presumably only in a perfectly competitive market, a rare if not endangered species). Rationality at the individual trucker and trader level has been reified to the wider higher-level society. It too, the larger economy and society, must be rational, and thereby predictable—that is, subject to the use of basic number-based formulae. The test of predictability comes from the numerous formulae that economists have created over time. Unfortunately, as noted above, quantitatively adept financial economists have had a questionable and contentious record on predicting market trends.

The Old Imperialists

The rationality assumption has traveled well throughout the social sciences. According to the Harvard University Press description of Nobel Prize winner Gary Becker's 1993 *A Treatise on the Family* [13]:

> Imagine each family as a kind of little factory...Becker applies economic theory to the most sensitive and fateful personal decisions, such as choosing a spouse or having children. He uses the basic economic assumptions of maximizing behavior, stable preferences, arid equilibria in explicit or implicit markets to analyze the allocation of time to child care as well as to careers, to marriage and divorce in polygynous as well as monogamous societies, to the increase and decrease of wealth from one generation to another...
>
> Becker extends the powerful tools of economic analysis to problems once considered the province of the sociologist, the anthropologist, and the historian. The obligation of these scholars to take account of his work thus constitutes an important step in the unification of the social sciences.
>
> *A Treatise on the Family* will have an impact on public policy as well. Becker shows that social welfare programs have significant effects on the allocation of resources within families. For example, social security taxes tend to reduce the amount of resources children give to their aged parents. The implications of these findings are obvious and far-reaching.

Fellow Freshwater Chicagoan, the brilliant Judge Richard A. Posner's 1983 *The Economics of Justice* applied economic theory to four areas of interest to students of social and legal institutions: [14]

> [His] book is designed to display the power of economics to organize and illuminate diverse fields in the study of nonmarket behavior and institutions. A central theme is the importance of uncertainty to an understanding of

social and legal institutions. Another major theme is that the logic of the law, in many ways but not all, appears to be an economic one: that judges, for example, in interpreting the common law, act as if they were trying to maximize economic welfare. (From the Harvard University Press description.)

Even non-Freshwater economists have found rationality a useful tool for understanding how societies are organized both for the good and for the bad. The remarkably inventive Mancur Olson, a leading figure in the New Institutional Economics, for example, introduced the concept of rational roving and stationary bandits:

> [U]nder anarchy, a 'roving bandit' only has the incentive to steal and destroy, whilst a 'stationary bandit'—a tyrant—has an incentive to encourage some degree of economic success as he expects to remain in power long enough to benefit from that success. A stationary bandit thereby begins to take on the governmental function of protecting citizens and their property against roving bandits. In the move from roving to stationary bandits, Olson sees the seeds of civilization, paving the way, eventually for democracy, which by giving power to those who align with the wishes of the population, improves incentives for good government.[15]

Both genres of bandits, Olson seems to suggest, roam freely in America today. He also predicted that rent-seeking and the increasing number of special interest groups pursuing their narrow self-interests will eventually lead to distributional conflict between the rich and the poor (represented by opposing political parties). This is another institutional economics version analogous to the work of John Kenneth Galbraith.

Again, one advantage of the rationality concept is that it invites analysts to formulate mathematical formulae and assign probabilities, important tools in the quest to understand both the past and the present.[16] Economics, as the earlier quotation from Larry Summers claimed, is a rule-based discipline: "[T]here are economic laws like there are physical laws, and as with physical laws, economic laws do not yield to political will." However, as noted in an earlier chapter, some economic historians have argued that one cannot use assumptions about rational economics in analyzing premodern economies. The infrastructure of useful economic laws can be questioned. Nor, according to Dani Rodrick, can we unquestionably use these assumptions elsewhere, as they imply (assume) a "perfectly competitive market world."[17]

Also again, do these laws rest on the assumption of a rational economic man?

We have already seen that behavioral economists suggest that such a man is on the endangered species list. Economists have recognized the sheet of sand on which rationality stands but have explained it away by hypothesizing that rational actions must be based on full and correct information. That can be a rare commodity; asymmetric information is common as well. Other critics suggest that one must factor in the relative influence (power) that competing truckers and traders have in pursuing their respective rational interests. Not all truckers and traders are equal, and the larger social system must be considered in formulating how markets operate—and how rational power can be used to create and sustain inequality.

Milton Friedman, as earlier noted, seems to have accepted that the rationality assumption was not an essential building block for economics—and, hence, for the social sciences more generally. Instead, if the formulae and models constructed by economists "work" fairly well in their predictive power, then it is not relevant whether economic man is rational or not. This suggests that the search for order, Heilbroner's understanding of what economists do, need not be based on the socially constructed concept of rationality. If the formulae work in some instances, then "maybe" that is enough to justify economics as a science. After all, quarks do not think and calculate. They just do what they do. No theology is required. The dictionaries of economic words, however, is infused with value assumptions, as suggested in our earlier review of how measures of national income are constructed and inequality is both explained and justified:

> Be wise now therefore, O ye kings: be instructed, ye judges of the earth.
>
> Why do the heathen rage, and the people imagine a vain thing?
>
> The kings of the earth take their stand and the rulers take counsel together against the Lord and against His Anointed, saying, "Let us tear their fetters apart and cast away their cords from us!"[18]

The end is not near, but this book is.

Notes

1. Critics of this assumption point to class (income) differences in multiplier effects. Wealthier truckers and traders are unable to spend all of their income and wealth, whereas the less fortunate are constrained to live within their means. The wealthy, as Keynes suggested, use their wealth to

play casino games that add to their own wealth but not the wealth of the nation. Say's law seems to assume that multiplier (aggregated at the national level) will never drop below 1.

2. The intersection of the "investment savings" (IS) and "liquidity preference–money supply" (LM) curves is the "general equilibrium," where there is simultaneous equilibrium in both markets. It is a major leap for noneconomists, such as the present noneconomist author, to move from this English-language description to an actual understanding of what the formula means and how to calculate it. Suffice it to note that the numbers used in this and other formulae are supposedly averages reflecting aggregated individual choices made by individual economic men at one particular time (and for other hypothesized times). Of course, various iterations of sensitivity analysis procedures (alternative assumptions) can be employed in using these and other formulae. See the opening reference to what is implied in an Alice-in-Wonderland world of economics.
3. Zachary Karabell, "The 'Laws of Economics' Don't Exist," *The Atlantic* (April 22, 2013).
4. His is not the only alternative to present perspectives. Chaos theories, e.g., provide another possible paradigm alternative to assumptions about rationality, predictability, and linear relationships. That kind of world does not easily fit with what George Creely, a progressive journalist, once wrote: "People do not live by bread alone: they live mostly by catch phrases," analogous to Kahneman's System 1 thinking.
5. Braudel has noted that "private markets did not arise merely to promote efficiency, but also to 'eliminate competition.'" Quoted in Wallerstein, op. cit., 211.
6. Robert K. Merton, "On Sociological Theories of the Middle Range," in his *Social Theory and Social Structure* (New York: Simon & Schuster, The Free Press, 1949) 39–53. Also in Calhoun, Craig et al *Classical Sociological Theory* (Boston: Wiley-Blackwell; 2 edition 2011): Chapter 35. Many economists would no doubt argue that their discipline already provides large numbers of useful middle-range theories. Merton's son Robert Cox Merton won the 1997 Nobel Memorial Prize in Economic Sciences.
7. From his entry in Brockman, op. cit., 317–18. He also wrote that "because economics and much of cognitive science take the unit of analysis to be an independent individual, they have difficulty accounting for such social [and economic] phenomena as financial bubbles, political movements, panics, technology trends, or even the course of scientific progress." Pentland and the other variations on traditional economics provide support for the title to his book, although it would be legitimate to add a few more words: *Inequality and the End of Economics as We Know It.* Milton Freidman, as suggested earlier, might have responded "so what?" If the mathematical formulae can make reasonable predictions, they can provide

a map of the present and an itinerary to the future. The distinction between prediction and explanation is interesting but not a necessary precondition for policy formulation. The formulae used to make predictions and forecasts meet Popper's criterion of falsifiability. Other philosophers of science might argue that there is an important difference between repeated patterns and the explanations for them. Patterns need not imply laws. Economists have been inventive in proposing numerous catchphrases that suggest underlying patterns and their causes—such as entropy, chaos, paradigms, and more. The discipline of economics, of course, is no different from other disciplines in the social and physical sciences.

8. The couplet "social physics" goes back to the Belgium scientist Lambert Adolphe Jacques Quételet's (1796–1874) use of mathematical principles to analyze numerical data as a way to better understand such phenomena as crime rates, marriage rates, or suicide rates. His concept of the "average man" (*l'homme moyen*) was characterized by the mean values of measured variables that follow a normal distribution. Auguste Comte (1798–1857) disagreed with Quételet's collection of statistics. He introduced the term "'sociologie" (sociology), also a number-based discipline adopted by Émile Durkheim (1858–1917) and the generations of sociologists who followed these early social physicists. Pentland's perspective has a long pedigree. Early in the 1960s, I cooperated with my University of California-Berkeley (UCB) colleagues in launching a social physics–type technological approach intended to help us better understand developments in China, a tightly controlled communist enclave at the time. Although the project was funded and resulted in some useful reports, our mining of mass amounts of printed newspaper archives was severely limited by (1) a lack of modern imagery technology that would have allowed us to convert Chinese characters into a searchable format, something the US postal service was in the process of developing for its own use, and (2) the absence of suitable translation software. For one of my own learning experiences from this work, see "Toward the Use of Content Analysis Procedures for Explanatory Studies," *Public Opinion Quarterly* (Summer, 1967), 230–241. Also "How Hong Kong Newspapers Have Responded to 15 Years of Rapid Social Change," *Asian Survey*, IX: 9 (September, 1969), 669–681. For the report on the UCB study, see Paul Wong, *China's Higher Leadership in the Socialist Transition* (Free Press, 1977). I lost track of this project when UCB loaned me to the new Chinese University of Hong Kong to establish its social research center.
9. Paul Krugman, "The M.I.T. Gang," online *New York Times* (July 24, 2015). As noted earlier, there are many schools of economics as well as competing mental models, as Rodrik covers in his previously referenced 2015 book.

10. Shiller, op. cit.
11. From my *A Concise History*.
12. Tim Harford, "The Wisdom of Crowds? A single economic forecast is usually wrong. But groups of economic forecasts are often just as mistaken. Why?" *Slate* (August 9, 2008) available online at http://www.slate.com/articles/arts/the_undercover_economist/2008/08/the_wisdom_of_crowds.single.html. Also see "Same as it ever was, What earlier banking crises reveal about America's travails today?" *Economist* (January 10, 2008) available online at http://www.economics.harvard.edu/files/faculty/51_What_Do_Earlier_Banking_Crises.pdf. Economists will (or should) remind us that they are dealing with "probabilities." "Sensitivity analysis" is one approach to display alternative "outcomes" based on changing or alternative assumptions. The use of multiple (alternative) models is another option. Neustadt and May, as noted earlier, are worth revisiting. They recommended that analysts supply their own assessments of their results and conclusions by assigning the odds they would give that their presumed results prove correct. How much of their own money would they wager on their prognosis? And they also suggest that the analysts indicate what fresh facts would cause the analysts to change their presumptions, choices, results, and recommendations.
13. http://www.hup.harvard.edu/catalog.php?isbn=9780674906990.
14. http://www.hup.harvard.edu/catalog.php?isbn=9780674235267.
15. Wikipedia entry. It goes on to note that "Olson founded the Center for Institutional Reform in the Informal Sector ("IRIS Center"), funded by USAID (United States Agency for International Development). Based at the University of Maryland, the Center sought to supply an intellectual foundation for legal and economic reform projects carried out by USAID in formerly communist states that were attempting to make the transition to market-driven democratic governments governed by the rule of law. It was particularly active in East and Central Europe and the former Soviet Union. Much of my career with USAID, many years before I met Mancur, was generally but not entirely built around his understanding of institutional economics. He and I worked within different environments: Mancur was a theorist. Because I was responsible for millions of American taxpayer dollars, it was essential that I be able to demonstrate that these dollars were having their intended consequences (as they did).
16. Logos, according to Bart Ehrman, can mean reason, something inherent in nature. Logic in this philosophical and religious sense need not imply truth nor determinism (predictability). Reason can be a social construct, whereas determinism lies more in the realm of mathematics.
17. Op. cit., 47.
18. Psalm 2:10.

Publications Cited

Akerlof, George A., and Robert J. Shiller. 2015. *Phishing for phools, The economics of manipulation and deception*. Princeton: Princeton University Press.

Allen, Katie. 2013. Nobel prize-winning economists take disagreement to whole new level. *The Guardian*, December 10.

Alonso, William, and Paul Starr. 1984. *The politics of numbers*. New York: Russell Sage Foundation.

Aslan, Reza. 2005. *No god but God. The origins, evolution, and future of Islam*. New York: Random House.

Atkinson, Anthony. 2015. *Inequality. What can be done*. Cambridge: Harvard University Press.

Banfield, Edward. 1958. *The moral basis of a backward society*. Glencoe: Free Press.

Becker, Gary. 1993. *A treatise on the family*. Cambridge: Harvard University Press.

Beneke, Chris. 2015. The myth of American religious coercion. 15(3), Spring. www.common-place.org

Boldizzoni, Francesco. 2011. *The poverty of Clio, resurrecting economic history*. Princeton: Princeton University Press.

Bourdieu, Pierre. 2007. The field of cultural production, or: The economic world reversed. In *Contemporary sociological theory*, reprinted in Craig Calhoun et al., eds. Oxford: Blackwell.

Commons, John. 1924. *Legal foundations of capitalism*. New York: Macmillan.

Coyle, Diane. 2014. *GDP, A brief affectionate history*. Princeton: Princeton University Press.

Curzan, Anne. 2015. A table alphabeticall. *Michigan Today*, August 18.

Daoud, Kamel. 2015. *Meursault investigation*. New York: Other Press.

Deaton, Angus. 2013. *The great escape: Health, wealth, and the origins of inequality*. Princeton: Princeton University Press.

© The Editor(s) (if applicable) and the Author(s) 2016
R.E. Mitchell, *The Language of Economics*,
DOI 10.1007/978-3-319-33981-8

Defoe, Daniel. 1719. *The life and strange surprizing adventures of Robinson Crusoe*. London: Printed for W. Taylor.
Defoe, Daniel. 1726. *The complete English tradesman*. London: Printed for Charles Rivington.
Easterly, Williams. 2015. *The tyranny of experts*. New York: Basic Books.
Ehrman, Bart A. 2005. *Misquoting Jesus*. New York: Harper.
Ehrman, Bart A. 2014. *How Jesus became God: The exaltation of a Jewish preacher from Galilee*. New York: HarperOne.
Eichengreen, Barry. 2013. Our children's economics. *Project Syndicate Blog*, February 11.
Ferguson, James. 1994. *The anti-politics machine*. Minneapolis: University of Minnesota Press.
Finkelstein, Israel, and Neil Asher Silberman. 2001. *The Bible unearthed: Archaeology's new vision of ancient Israel and the origin of its sacred texts*. New York: Simon & Schuster.
Fischer, David Hackett. 1970. *Historians' fallacies: Toward a logic of historical thought*. New York: Harper & Row.
Freedman, Lawrence. 2013. *Strategy, A history*. Oxford: Oxford University Press.
Friedman, Milton. 1953. *Essays in positive economics*. Chicago: University of Chicago Press.
Galbraith, John Kenneth. 1952. *American capitalism: The concept of countervailing power*. Boston: Houghton Mifflin.
Galbraith, John Kenneth. 1967. *The new industrial state*. Boston: Houghton Mifflin.
Gray, John. 2015. *The soul of the marionette, A short inquiry into human freedom*. New York: Farrar, Straus and Giroux.
Harford, Tim. 2008. The wisdom of crowds? A single economic forecast is usually wrong. But groups of economic forecasts are often just as mistaken. Why? *Slate*, August 9.
Heilbroner, Robert. 1999. *The worldly philosophers: The lives, times and ideas of the great economic thinkers*, 7th edn. Touchstone Paperback.
Hidalgo, Cesar, quoted in John Brockman, (ed.). 2015. *This idea must die, scientific theories that are blocking progress*. Toronto: Harper.
Himmelfarb, Gertrude. 2008. *The roads to modernity, The British, French and American enlightenments*. London: Vintage.
James Gleick, *Chaos: Making a New Science* (Penguin, 2008).
Kahneman, Daniel. 2011. *Thinking fast and slow*. New Yor: Farrar, Straus and Giroux.
Karabell, Zachary 2013. The 'laws of economics' don't exist. *The Atlantic*, April 22.
Krugman, Paul. 1994. *Peddling prosperity*. New York: Norton.
Krugman, Paul. 2009. How did economists get it so wrong? *New York Times Magazine*, September 2.

Krugman, Paul. 2015. The M.I.T. Gang. online *New York Times,* July 24.
Kuhn, Thomas. 1962. *The structure of scientific revolutions.* Chicago: University of Chicago.
Lazarsfeld, Paul F., and Raymond Boudon. 1993. *On social research and its language.* Chicago: University of Chicago Press.
Llewellyn, Karl N. 2008. *The bramble bush, The classic lectures on the law and law school.* Oxford: Oxford University Press.
Loomis, Carol J. 2012. Should you leave it all to the children? *Fortune,* November 21.
Lucas, Robert. 2014. The industrial revolution: Past and present. 2003 Annual Report Essay, Federal Reserve Bank of Minneapolis, May 1.
Malthus, Thomas, 1798. *An Essay on the principle of population, as it affects the future improvement of society with remarks on the speculations of Mr. Godwin, M. Condorcet, and other writers.* Anonymously published (1798) with later editions ending in 1839.
Mandeville, Bernard. 1714. *Fable of the bees* (later versions).
Manza, Jeff. 2015. Reconnecting the political and the economic in the new gilded age. *Contemporary Sociology,* July.
Marshall, Alfred. 1890. *Principles of economics.* New York: Macmillan.
Martin, Dale. 2004. *Inventing superstition, From the Hippocratics to the Christians.* Cambridge: Harvard University Press.
McCloskey, Deirdre N. 1998. *The rhetoric of economics.* Madison: University of Wisconsin.
McCloskey, Deirdre N. 2014. *Bourgeois dignity: Why economics can't explain the modern world.* Chicago: University of Chicago Press.
McMahon, Darrin M., and Samuel Moyn (eds.). 2014. *Rethinking modern European intellectual history.* Oxford: Oxford University Press.
Merton, R.K. 1949. On sociological theories of the middle range. In *Social theory and social structure,* ed. R.K. Merton. New York: Simon & Schuster/The Free Press.
Merton, Robert K., With George Reader, and Patricia Kendall. 1975. *The student-physician: Introductory studies in the sociology of medical education.* Cambridge: Harvard University Press.
Merton, Robert K., With Elinor Barber. 2006. *The travels and adventures of serendipity: A study in sociological semantics and the sociology of science.* Princeton: Princeton University Press.
Michels, Robert. 1911. *Political parties: A sociological study of the oligarchical tendencies of modern democracy political parties.* Free Press; 2nd Free Press Paperback Edition 1968 edition (April 1, 1966)
Mill, John Stewart. 1848. *Principles of political economy.* London: John W. Parker.
Mitchell, Robert E. 1966. Polity, church attractiveness, and ministers' careers: An eight denomination study of inter-church mobility. *Journal for the Scientific Study of Religion* 5 (Spring): 241–258.

Mitchell, Robert E. 1967. Toward the use of content analysis procedures for explanatory studies. *Public Opinion Quarterly*, Summer, 230–241.

Mitchell, Robert E. 1969. How Hong Kong newspapers have responded to 15 years of rapid social change. *Asian Survey*, IX: 9 (September).

Mitchell, Robert E. 1973. Survey materials collected in the developing countries: Sampling, measurement, and interviewing obstacles to intra-and inter-national comparisons. In *International Social Science Journal*, 17(4): 1965 and reprinted variously including in Donald Warwick and Samuel Osherson, eds., *Comparative Research Methods*. Englewood Cliffs: Prentice-Hall.

Mitchell, Robert E. 2007. Donald Tsang's proposed family policycCommission: Lessons from Hong Kong and American experiences. *The Hong Kong Journal of Social Work*, 41(1 & 2): 81–94, summer and winter.

Mitchell, Robert E. 2014. *A concise history of economists' assumptions about markets: From Adam Smith to Joseph Schumpeter*. Praeger: Santa Barbara.

Morris, Ian. 2015. To each age its inequality. *New York Times Opinion Pages*, July 9.

Nasar, Sylvia. 2011. *Grand pursuit: The story of economic genius*. New York: Simon & Schuster.

Neustadt, Richard E., and Ernest R. May. 1986. *Thinking in time: The uses of history for decision makers*. New York: Free Press.

Orwell, George. 1949. *Nineteen eighty-four*. London: Secker & Warburg.

Pentland, Alex. 2014. *Social physics*. New York: The Penguin Press.

Phillips, Kevin. 2003. *Wealth and democracy: A political history of the American rich*. New York: Broadway Books.

Piketty, Thomas. 2013. *Capital in the twenty-first century*. Cambridge, MA: The Belknap Press of Harvard University Press.

Pine, B.J., and J.H. Gilmore. 1999. *The experience economy: Work is theatre every business a stage*. Boston: Harvard Business School Press.

Polanyi, Karl. 1957. *The great transformation: The political and economic origins of our time*. Boston: Beacon Press.

Poovey, Mary. 1998. *A history of the modern fact: Problems of knowledge in the sciences of wealth and society*. Chicago: University of Chicago Press.

Poovey, Mary. 2008. *Genres of the credit economy: Mediating value in eighteenth- and nineteenth-century Britain*. Chicago: University of Chicago Press.

Posner, Richard A. 1983. *The economics of justice*. Cambridge, MA: Harvard University Press.

Prasad, Monica. 2012. *A land of too much*. Cambridge, MA: Harvard University Press.

Princeton, 2014. The trouble with GDP. *The Economist* 2016.

Rawls, John. 1971. *A theory of justice*. Cambridge, MA: Belknap Press of Harvard University Press.

Rodrik, Dani. 2015. *Economics rules: The rights and wrongs of the dismal science*. New York: Norton.

Sahlins, Marshall. 1974. *Stone age economics*. New Brunswick, New Jersey – Rutgers College: Aldine Transaction.

Sahlins, Marshall. 2008. *The Western illusion of human nature: With reflections on the long history of hierarchy, equality and the sublimation of anarchy in the West, and … Conceptions of the human condition*. Chicago: Prickly Paradigm Press.

Samuels, Warren. 2011. *Erasing the invisible hand, essays on the elusive and misused concepts in economics*. Cambridge/New York: Cambridge University Press.

Sandel, Michael J. 2009. *Justice, what's the right thing to do*. New York: Farrar, Straus and Giroux.

Sandel, Michael J. 2012. *What money can't buy: The moral limits of markets*. New York: Farrar, Straus and Giroux.

Sawhill, Isabel. 2015. Whatever happened to middle class income gains?" July 7, Brookings Blog.

Schlefer, Jonathan. 2012. *The assumptions economists make*. Cambridge, MA: Belknap Press of Harvard University Press.

Schui, Florian. 2015. *Austerity: The great failure*. New Haven: Yale University Press.

Sewall Jr., William H. 2005. *Logics of history: Social theory and social transformation*, Chicago Studies in Practices of Meaning. Chicago: University of Chicago Press.

Shiller, Robert. 2015a. What good are economists. *Project Syndicate*, January 15.

Shiller, Robert. 2015b. The housing market still isn't rational. *New York Times*, July 26.

Smith, Adam. 1759. *The theory of moral sentiments*. London: A. Kincaid and J. Bell.

Smith, Adam. 1776. *An inquiry into the nature and causes of the wealth of nations*. London: W. Strahan and T. Cadell.

Stark, Rodney, and Roger Finke. 2005. *The churching of America 1776–2005: Winners and losers in our religious economy*. New Brunswick: Rutgers University Press.

Stiglitz, Joseph. 2002. Celebrating the irrational. *Project Syndicate*, December 11.

Stiglitz, Joseph. 2015. *The great divide, Unequal societies and what we can do about them*. New York: Norton.

Summers, Larry. 2015. Incrementalism won't cure these crises. *Washington Post Op-Ed*, July 12.

The New Palgrave Dictionary of Economics (Palgrave Macmillan, 2008).

The Oxford Dictionary of Economics (Oxford University Press, 2009).

The Oxford Dictionary of World Religions (1997).

Turner, James. 2014. *Phi.lo.o.gy: 1. The forgotten origins of the modern humanities*. Princeton: Princeton University Press.

Wallerstein, Immanuel. 2001. *The limits of nineteenth-century paradigms: Unthinking social science*, 2nd ed. Philadelphia: Temple.

Warsh, David. 2007. *Knowledge and the wealth of nations: A story of economic discovery*. New York: Norton.

Wile, Rob. Robert Shiller Debunks Eugene Fama's ideas to his face during this Nobel Prize presentation. Available online at: http://www.businessinsider.com/robert-shiller-nobel-presentation-2013-12?op=1#ixzz3fFoJD4oV.

Wolff, Edward, and Maury, Gittleman. 2011. *Inheritances and the distribution of wealth or whatever happened to the great inheritance boom?* U.S, Bureau of Labor Statistics, Working Paper 44, January 5.

Wong, Paul. 1977. *China's higher leadership in the socialist transition.* New York: Free Press.

Zetterberg, Hans. 2009. *The many-splendored society: Surrounded by symbols.* Scotts Valley: CreateSpace.

Index

© The Editor(s) (if applicable) and the Author(s) 2016

R.E. Mitchell, *The Language of Economics*,
DOI 10.1007/978-3-319-33981-8

M

N

O

T

U

V

The manufacturer's authorised representative in the EU is Springer Nature Customer Service Centre GmbH, Europaplatz 3, 69115 Heidelberg, Germany. If you have any concerns regarding our products, please contact ProductSafety@springernature.com

Printed and bound by CPI Group (UK) Ltd, Croydon, CR0 4YY
01/10/2026
02225978-0008